THE ORTHODOX BI
S

UNIVERSAL TRUTH

THE CATHOLIC EPISTLES
OF JAMES, PETER, JUDE, AND JOHN

by Fr. Lawrence R. Farley

Ancient Faith Publishing
Chesterton, Indiana

Dedicated to
Prof. Albert Pietersma, scholar and teacher,
solver of Greek mysteries,
and friend to his aging students

Table of Contents and Outline

The Second Epistle of St. John

The Third Epistle of St. John

Excurses:

❧ Introduction to the Series ❧

A Word about Scholarship and Translation

This commentary was written for your grandmother. And for your plumber, your banker, your next-door neighbor, and the girl who serves you French fries at the nearby McDonald's. That is, it was written for the average layman, for the nonprofessional who feels a bit intimidated by the presence of copious footnotes, long bibliographies, and all those other things which so enrich the lives of academics. It is written for the pious Orthodox layman who is mystified by such things as Source Criticism, but who nonetheless wants to know what the Scriptures mean.

Therefore, it is unlike many other commentaries, which are written as contributions to the ongoing endeavor of scholarship and as parts of a continuous dialogue among scholars. That endeavor and dialogue is indeed worthwhile, but the present commentary forms no part of it. For it assumes, without argument, a certain point of view, and asserts it without defense, believing it to be consistent with the presuppositions of the Fathers and therefore consistent with Orthodox Tradition. It has but one aim: to be the sort of book a busy parish priest might put in the hands of an interested parishioner who says to him over coffee hour after Liturgy, "Father, I'm not sure I really get what St. Paul is saying in the Epistles. What does it all mean?" This commentary tries to tell the perplexed parishioner what the writers of the New Testament mean.

Regarding the translation used herein, an Italian proverb says, "All translators are traitors." (The proverb proves its own point, for it sounds better in Italian!) The point of the proverb, of course, is that no translation, however careful, can bring out all the nuances and meanings of the original, since no language can be the mathematical equivalent of another. The English translator is faced, it would seem, with a choice: either he can make the translation something of a rough paraphrase of the original and render it into flowing sonorous English; or he can attempt to make a fairly literal, word-for-word translation from the original with the resultant English being stilted, wooden, and clumsy.

These two basic and different approaches to translation correspond to two basic and different activities in the Church. The Church needs a translation of the Scriptures for use in worship. This should be in good, grammatical, and flowing English, as elegant as possible and suited to its function in the majestic worship of the Liturgy. The Church also needs a translation of the Scriptures for private study and for group Bible study. Here the elegance of its English is of lesser concern. What is of greater concern here is the bringing out of all the nuances found in the original. Thus this approach will tend to sacrifice elegance for literality and, wherever possible, seek a word-for-word correspondence with the Greek. Also, because the student will want to see how the biblical authors use a particular word (especially St. Paul, who has many works included in the canon), a consistency of translation will be sought and the same Greek word will be translated, wherever possible, by the same English word or by its cognate.

The present work does not pretend to be anything other than a translation for private Bible study. It seeks to achieve, as much as possible, a literal, word-for-word correspondence with the Greek. The aim has been to present a translation from which one could jump back into the Greek original with the aid of an interlinear New Testament. Where a single Greek word has been used in the original, I have tried to find (or invent!) a single English word.

The result, of course, is a translation so literally rendered from the Greek that it represents an English spoken nowhere on the planet! That is, it represents a kind of "study Bible English" and not an actual vernacular. It was never intended for use outside the present commentaries, much less in the worship of the Church. The task of producing a flowing, elegant translation that nonetheless preserves the integrity and nuances of the original I cheerfully leave to hands more competent than mine.

Key to the Format of This Work:

• The translated text is first presented in boldface type. Italics within these biblical text sections represent words required by English syntax that are not actually present in the Greek. Each translated text section is set within a shaded grey box.

> ❧ ❧ ❧ ❧ ❧
>
> 13 Come now, you who say, "Today or tomorrow we will go into this or that city, and do *business for* a year there and trade and *make a* profit."
> 14 You do not understand what your life *will be* tomorrow. You are a vapor that appears for a little *while* and then disappears.

• In the commentary sections, citations from the portion of text being commented upon are given in boldface type.

If persecution, hardship, or sickness have driven **anyone** of them from God, so that one **strays from the truth** of the Gospel, they should do all things possible to win him back.

• In the commentary sections, citations from other locations in Scripture are given in quotation marks with a reference; any reference not including a book name refers to the book under discussion.

The word translated *peer* is the Greek *parakupto*, translated "to stoop" in John 20:11.

• In the commentary sections, italics are used in the ordinary way—for emphasis, foreign words, etc.

The word rendered *marvelous* is the Greek *thaumastos*, cognate with *thauma*, "wonder, miracle."

❧ The General Epistle of St. James ❧

Introduction

The Epistle of James has, to some degree, suffered the fate of Jewish Christianity itself. That is, it has come to be somewhat misunderstood, devalued, and forgotten. Just as Gentile Christian churches soon outnumbered Jewish Christian churches, so that Christianity soon came to be thought of as a Gentile phenomenon, so the epistles of Paul came to outshine the homely epistle of James.

Thinking of Paul's letters, some have assumed that an epistle must be filled with doctrinal teaching, expounding on the nature of Christ and salvation, wrestling with the great philosophical rivals of the day. Such people have looked with disappointment for such things in the Epistle of James, and have therefore tended to put it on the shelf. The most outstanding example of such misunderstanding and devaluation is that of Martin Luther, who denounced James as "an epistle of straw," the work of a mischievous non-Christian Jew, because he could not find in it his pet teaching, "justification by faith alone."

Such misunderstanding (not confined to the German reformer) is unfortunate. When the Epistle of James is not read through such biased lenses, but is allowed to speak for itself, it shines as a great treasure and a much-needed prophetic and pastoral word.

Who was this James? Tradition ascribes the epistle to James, the brother of Jesus. He presided over the mother church in Jerusalem as its first bishop (see Acts 12:17; 15:13f), and since Jerusalem exercised a central role in coordinating Christian missions, his pastoral authority extended well beyond the flock of the city itself. Just as all Jewish Christians of the first century looked to Jerusalem as the mother church, so they would have to some degree looked to James for moral leadership. Indeed, when Jude came to write his own epistle later in that century, it was enough for him to refer to himself as "the brother of James" (Jude 1) to establish his own authority. After serving as bishop to the Christian community, James ended his days as a martyr in about the year 62, being thrown down from the temple parapet and clubbed to death as he preached to the people about Jesus.

James presided over an essentially Jewish Christianity. Indeed, in his day, the dividing line between Judaism and Christianity was not well drawn, and even St. Paul could tell his Jewish brothers in Rome that he was in Roman bonds and was suffering "for the sake of the hope of Israel" (Acts 28:20). The division was then between those Jews who saw in Jesus the fulfillment of their national and ancestral hopes, and those Jews who regarded Him simply as a blaspheming deceiver. The Christian Jews, those who believed in Jesus as the Messiah, still regarded themselves as good Jews, and as such would have kept all the Jewish customs, such as Sabbath, circumcision, temple worship, and the food laws.

This division, though between Jew and Jew, was still drawn firmly enough. Indeed, those who rejected Jesus tended to persecute their Jewish brothers who did believe, the most famous example of which was the stoning of Stephen in the mid-thirties and the subsequent scattering of the Jerusalem church. The writer to the Hebrews (though writing somewhat later) speaks of believers being arrested and having their property seized (Heb. 10:34). The people to whom James wrote his epistle were those familiar with persecution and trial (see James 1:12; 2:6–7). Some were rich landowners (a fixture in pre-AD 70 Palestine), but most were not.

These people faced the temptation not to live out their faith in Jesus, but instead to fall back into worldly ways, pursuing wealth, quarreling with their brethren, judging and reproaching the poor. Enamored of worldly status, many wanted to become teachers, elders in the Christian community, in order to further their ambition. Some of the poor suffered hardship at the hands of the rich landowners whose lands they worked.

It was to these that James wrote, offering pastoral words of rebuke and encouragement. His epistle insists that true Christian faith is actualized in works, foremost of which is control of the tongue. Just as the chief priest in Jerusalem might send out letters to the Jewish Diaspora, so as pastor of the mother church James sent out this letter to Jewish Christians everywhere, as a kind of encyclical sermon. (Apart from the opening greeting, James's letter does not bear any other epistolary characteristics.)

He wrote at a time when the Church was still almost entirely Jewish (witness the fact that the gatherings of the Christians were still called "synagogues" [Gr. *sunagoge*, James 2:2]; the other term for gathering, *ecclesia* or "church," had not yet won the currency it was later to have). Since Paul's first missionary journey began about AD 47, and Gentile churches began to proliferate in the early 50s, it seems that James wrote his epistle shortly before this, at about AD 48, from Jerusalem.

The quality of the Greek is very polished, and it is possible that James used an amanuensis. (Indeed, St. Jerome, in his *Lives of Illustrious Men*, mentions that the epistle "is even claimed by some to have been published by some one else under [James's] name," and perhaps this ancient guess reflects the presence of such an amanuensis.) But many Jews raised in Galilee spoke excellent Greek as well, and such polished Greek need not necessarily have been beyond James's literary reach.

Though undervalued by some (it was late securing a place in the New Testament canon), the Epistle of James remains in the Church, an authentic apostolic voice from the early dawn of the Church's life.

℘ The Epistle of St. James ℘

Opening Greetings (1:1)

---

1 1   James, a slave of God and of the Lord Jesus
Christ, to the twelve tribes in the Diaspora,
greetings.

In the opening greeting with which epistles began in that day,
James begins by describing himself as **a slave of God**. This was a title
of honor, for it establishes him as one who waits upon God, with
all the closeness of a slave to his master. (Kings, such as David, were
sometimes given this title; see 1 Kg. 8:66 LXX.) More remarkable
is James's reference to himself as the slave **of the Lord Jesus Christ**.
Though James was His brother (i.e. kinsman), Jesus had been exalted
as Lord and Christ over all, and ties of blood and kinship were now
utterly irrelevant. James's boast is not that he was Jesus' brother or
kinsman. It is that he remains until that hour His true slave.

James addresses his letter **to the twelve tribes in the Diaspora**.
The Diaspora was an abiding reality for Israel, and it referred to the
Jews scattered throughout the world (see John 7:35). James thus
intends his letter to have the widest possible distribution: it is not
simply for his own flock in Jerusalem, but for Jewish Christians
throughout the world, wherever they may be. The reference to **the
twelve tribes** is a way of indicating totality (compare Paul's use of
the term in Acts 26:7)—all the believers in Christ are included. (At
the time of writing, there were no non-Jewish believers in Christ to
speak of; all the Church was still Jewish.) Though in the mouth of
a non-Christian Jew, the term "the twelve tribes" meant "all racial

Israel," in the mouth of a Christian like James it seems clear that he was addressing all (Jewish) believers in Jesus. Jews who did not believe in Him were outside his literary purview. This is because for James, the disciples of Jesus were the true Israel, inheritors of the hope promised in the Law and the Prophets, and those Jews who rejected Jesus forfeited their heritage as Jews.

Unlike Paul and Peter after him, James does not expand his literary opening beyond the required **greetings**. It is interesting to see that the epistle written from the Council of Jerusalem (quoted in Acts 15:23–29) and probably written by James, has the same terse opening, "greetings." This tends to confirm the view that the author of this epistle is the same one who was leader of the Jerusalem Church and presided over that council.

§II. Exhortation to Endure under Trial (1:2–18)

≷ ≷ ≷ ≷ ≷

2 Esteem *it* all joy, my brothers, whenever you fall into various testings,

3 knowing that the proving of your faith works perseverance.

4 And let perseverance have its perfect work, that you may be perfect and intact, lacking in nothing.

5 But if anyone of you lacks wisdom, let him ask from God, who gives to all men generously and without reproaching, and it will be given to him.

6 But let him ask in faith, without any wavering, for the one who wavers is like a wave of the sea, wind-driven and tossed.

7 For let not that man suppose that he will receive anything from the Lord,

8 being a double-souled man, restless in all his ways.

St. James writes to his fellow disciples of Jesus, calling them **brothers**. This is an important word in this epistle, for James uses it as an affectionate term of address fifteen times. This shows that he addresses his hearers, not as an exalted judge, but as a fellow believer (compare Matt. 23:8), appealing to them to submit to the same teaching to which he himself submits, even though he is the leader of the community. The entire epistle breathes this free air of Christian egalitarianism.

James first speaks to those who are under **various testings**. The word rendered *testing* is the Greek *peirasmos*, used for a trial of suffering so severe that it could cause one to fall away from one's faith. It was from this experience of testing that Christ urged His disciples in Gethsemane to pray that God would deliver them and bring them safely through (Mark 14:38). James uses the word here to describe the various and many ways in which the Christian Jews are persecuted by their non-Christian neighbors. They may be tempted to despair and conclude that God has abandoned them.

Not so, says James. Such persecutions are not a catastrophe. Instead, his readers should **esteem *it* all joy** and nothing but joy **whenever** they suffer for their faith, **knowing that the proving of** their **faith** in the furnace of persecution **works perseverance** and steadfastness into their hearts. They should not find ways of compromising their faith in Christ to avoid suffering, but instead **let perseverance have its perfect work** (Gr. *teleion ergon*). Let the experience of enduring persecution do its job of purifying the heart. Then the believer will be **perfect and intact**.

The words rendered *perfect* and *intact* are the Greek *teleios* and *olokleros*. The word *teleios* here means not so much sinless as mature, blameless, completely dedicated. It corresponds with the Hebrew word *tam*, used in Genesis 6:9 to describe Noah in his dedication to God. The word *olokleros* means whole, entire, not fractured by divided loyalties. The Psalmist prayed that God would unite his heart that he might fear His Name (Ps. 86:11), and James says that enduring persecution with joy results finally in having a united heart, one zealously set on serving God, so that one is **lacking in nothing** that one needs.

Some, however, may think they **lack wisdom** so that they do not know how to respond to persecution. What should they say when they are challenged about their faith? How should they respond to being insulted and dragged into court? Such need only **ask from God**, and such wisdom **will be given**. God is not stingy with His gifts. He is the One **who gives to all men generously**, spontaneously, openly (Gr. *aplos*), the One who gives **without reproaching** His children for their poverty and their mistakes. If they ask God, He will give them all the wisdom they need to respond to each situation.

But **let** the petitioner **ask in faith, without any wavering, for the one who wavers is like a wave of the sea, wind-driven and tossed. Let not** such a **man** as that **suppose that he will receive anything from the Lord.** The word *waver* here indicates not so much the element of *psychological* hesitancy as it does the element of *moral* hesitancy. The waverer here is not one who needs *mental certainty* that his prayer will be answered. He needs *moral decisiveness* in his approach to God; he needs to repent of being **double-souled** (Gr. *dipsuchos*), of trying to live both as a worldling and as God's servant at the same time. The doubter has no moral stability, but is like a surging **wave of the sea, wind-driven and tossed** by his passions. **In all his ways** and dealings, he is **restless** and unreliable. The one who is not decided in his choice to serve God and not the world can never receive such wisdom from God. Persecution will find him out for what he is, and he will be at a loss.

❧ ❧ ❧ ❧ ❧

9 But let the lowly brother boast in his exaltation,

10 and the rich one *boast* in his lowliness, because like a flower of the grass he will pass away.

11 For the sun rises with the burning *heat* and dries up the grass; and its flower falls off, and the beauty of its appearance perishes; thus also the rich one in his goings will wither.

Persecution reveals for the Christian the true state of things, stripping away the lies and illusions of the world. **The lowly brother**, the one who is poor in the world's goods, can **boast in his exaltation**, rejoicing in how God has chosen the poor to be rich in salvation, bypassing those rich who are wise in their own eyes (see Matt. 5:3; Luke 10:21; 1 Cor. 1:27–28). The persecutors may despoil him of his goods, but he has little to lose, and no persecution can take away his true riches, which await him in heaven (Matt. 6:19–21). The time of trial serves only to reveal the exaltation of the lowly.

Similarly, persecution reveals the true state of **the rich** brother also. This one can *boast* **in his lowliness**, since persecution reveals how transient and ephemeral earthly riches really are. When he is despoiled, it is a vivid reminder that he should not trust in his riches, but in God, for all will eventually die and leave their wealth behind. **The rich one, in** the midst of **his goings**, pursuits and business deals, eventually **will wither**, sicken and die. He will be just like the **flower of the grass**—beautiful while it lasts, but **the sun rises with the burning *heat*** and scorching wind **and dries up** all before it, so that its bloom soon **falls off** and all its **beauty perishes**. For all his show of glory and permanence, the rich man is still transient as the grass, and the time of trial reveals his essential lowliness to him—to his great spiritual benefit.

꧁ ꧁ ꧁ ꧁ ꧁

12 Blessed *is* the man who perseveres *under* testing; for when he has been approved, he will receive the crown of life, which He has promised to those who love Him.

13 Let no one say when he is tested, "I am being tested by God," for God is not tested by wickedness, and He Himself tests no one.

14 But each one is tested when he is drawn away and lured by his own desire.

15 Then when desire has conceived, it brings forth sin; and when sin is finished, it brings forth death.

16 Do not be deceived, my beloved brothers.
17 For all good giving and every perfect gift is from above, coming down from the Father of lights, with whom there is no change or shadow of turning.
18 Having intended *it*, He brought us forth by the Word of truth, that we might be a sort of firstfruits of His creatures.
19 *This* you know, my beloved brothers.

James then pronounces the man **blessed** who **perseveres** *under* **testing** and holds to his faith. After **he has been approved** and has stood the test, on the Last Day **he will receive the crown** as a reward for that faithfulness—eternal **life** in the age to come, which the Lord **has promised to those who love Him**. Here is the final incentive to persevere and rejoice under trial.

For of course there are other possible responses to such suffering. One might **say when he is** so **tested, "I am being tested by God"**— "God is angry with me, and sends this catastrophe to destroy me." To blame God for one's suffering is a perennial temptation to the human heart, but it is a mistake. For **God** Himself **is not tested by wickedness**. Evil and malice find no place in Him, and He is not tempted to vengefulness as men are. No one must imagine that his sins have so exasperated God that He is now overcome with the all-too-human desire for retribution, and that this is the cause of his suffering. He **tests no one** like that, out of a desire to destroy them.

Rather, the spiritual danger in all our times of trial and suffering comes from our own fallenness. **Each one is tested** and tempted (the verb *peirazo* means both "to test" and "to tempt") **when he is drawn away** from safety **and lured** into danger **by his own desire**. For in each of us lives fallen **desire** (Gr. *epithumia*, usually used in a negative sense, and sometimes translated "lust"). This inner darkness manifests itself in willfulness, in rebellious determination to have our own way, and in uncontrollable appetites. Outer experiences of suffering usually bring this inner darkness to the fore and cause us to rage against God, but it is this inner darkness, not the outward suffering, that is the danger to us and is to blame. Testing and suffering are only spiritually dangerous because we are fallen.

This **desire** therefore must be resisted at all costs. For when it **has conceived, it brings forth** and gives birth to **sin**, and **when sin is finished** and mature, **it brings forth death**. Our desires and self-will may seem harmless, but they are lethal.

James addresses his flock as his **beloved brothers** and tenderly urges them **not** to **be deceived** into thinking God does not love them. God does not allow testing and persecution so that we may fail, but so that we may succeed and become seasoned, proven, holy. He gives only good things. Indeed, **all good giving and every perfect gift is from above, coming down from the Father of lights**. Every blessing in life we receive—health, love, friendship, pleasure, peace—all come ultimately from the decrees of God in heaven. He is **the Father of lights**, the Creator of the sun, moon, and stars that adorn the heavens. The Creator of such beauty could only will good for us. And the Creator of such heavenly lights is Himself Light. The lights of heaven may change, as day gives way to night, or as an eclipse obscures the light. But God's light and love never change, never dim, are never obscured. With Him **there is no change or shadow** due to **turning**.

As proof of this, James recalls what God freely and deliberately **intended** for us in Christ. Though under no compulsion, God yet **brought us forth by the Word of Truth** (the proclaimed Gospel), giving birth to us as His children, **that we might be a sort of firstfruits of His creatures**. He did not have to save us, but He did. (The verb rendered *brought forth*, Gr. *apokueo*, usually refers to a mother giving birth; compare its use in v. 15. The reference here is to our new birth in the waters of baptism.) At the end, He will transfigure the entire cosmos. But for now, He has transfigured us, as the **firstfruits** and pledge of what He will do for all His **creatures**, His entire creation. St. James reminds his readers that their exalted status as God's firstfruits is no novel teaching. He is simply exhorting them to live consistently with what they already **know**.

§III.   Exhortation to Be Doers of the Word (1:19—2:26)

> ﾞﾞ ﾞﾞ ﾞﾞ ﾞﾞ ﾞﾞ
>
> 19 But let every man be quick to hear, slow to speak, slow to wrath,
> 20 for the wrath of man does not work the righteousness of God.
> 21 Therefore putting off all filthiness and abundance of wickedness, in meekness welcome the implanted Word, which is able to save your souls.

Times of persecution and stress can tempt one to be overly defensive to everyone, to angrily shout back before hearing what the other person has said, and to harbor hostility when all is over. Instead of this, James says that **every man** must be **quick to hear, slow to speak,** and **slow to wrath**. The exhortation echoes the counsel found in Sirach 5:11, "Be quick to hear, deliberate in answering." One must let the other person finish his say, weigh a response carefully before responding, and not instantly turn **to wrath,** nurturing anger in one's heart.

The word rendered *wrath* is the Greek *orge*, used not so much for sudden outbursts but for smoldering resentment, enduring antagonism. One must resist such a passion, **for the wrath of man does not work the righteousness of God**. God will indeed establish His **righteousness** and His Kingdom on the earth (compare Matt. 3:15 for such a use of the term "righteousness"); He will overcome those that oppress the Christians and will vindicate the truth. But it is self-evident that **the wrath of man** cannot further such purposes, however much zealots may think otherwise. Christians need not angrily defend themselves. Let them give place to God's judgment (Rom. 12:19).

The task of Christians is **therefore** to **put off all** moral **filthiness and abundance of wickedness**, the sordid depravity with which the world overflows. They must decisively reject whatever evil remains from their old life. The verb rendered *put off* is in the aorist tense, indicating a single, energetic decision. Theirs is not to be a half-hearted rejection of evil, but a vigorous once-for-all commitment to holiness. This will be possible as they **in meekness welcome the implanted Word**.

This **Word** is the word of teaching given by their teachers and elders, who expound the Scriptures and transmit the counsels of Christ (such as those in His Sermon on the Mount). They are to listen to their teachers **in meekness**, tremblingly **welcoming** the teaching into their inner hearts, humbly accepting correction, and eagerly looking for opportunities to hear such exhortations. This Word will thus be **implanted** within them and will bear the fruit of a transformed life. It is not to be received as Christian entertainment, but as that which is **able to save** their **souls**, as the instrument of God for their final salvation. No wonder they should welcome it and look for opportunities to receive it.

---

৯৯ ৯৯ ৯৯ ৯৯ ৯৯

22 Become doers of the Word, and not hearers only, deluding yourselves.

23 For if anyone is a hearer of the Word and not a doer, this one is like a man who considers the face of his birth in a mirror;

24 for he has considered himself and gone away, and has immediately forgotten what he was like.

25 But one who peers into the perfect Law, the *Law* of freedom, and remains alongside *it*, not having become a forgetful hearer but a doer of work, this one will be blessed in his doing.

26 If anyone thinks *himself* to be religious, and yet does not bridle his tongue but deceives his heart, this one's religion *is* useless.

27 Religion pure and undefiled before God, even the Father, is this: to visit orphans and widows in their tribulation, and to keep oneself unstained from the world.

If they will do this, they will **become doers of the Word, and not hearers only**. To be a hearer only was ever the temptation of the Jews. The Torah was such a wonderful divine gift that some Jews thought it was enough to be a hearer of the Law to be justified (compare Rom. 2:13). But the Law was only given so that it might be carried out in one's daily life. If one thinks merely hearing it is enough, he is **deluding** himself and will learn the immensity of his folly at the Last Judgment.

For to be **a hearer of the Word**, to listen to the teachers expound on how one should live, and then to not fulfill it, is folly indeed. It is as ridiculous as a man who **considers** his **face in a mirror** in order to see where he needs to wash, and then having looked, **goes away**, having **immediately forgotten what he was like**, without washing. (The man's face is called **the face of his birth** to stress that he was born with this face, and knows exactly what it should look like—and therefore at a glance knows where it needs to be washed.) With typically Jewish humor, James paints a picture of a man who checks himself in a mirror and then rushes off, doing nothing about what he has just seen. Surely one looks in the mirror for the purpose of washing off whatever dirt is there? In the same way, a man only hears the Word in order to improve his life and repent of whatever the teaching instructs him to repent of.

Instead of imitating the man who ridiculously looks at his face and then forgets it, the Christian must **peer** intently **into the perfect Law**, the teaching of the Christian elders that brings **freedom**. The word translated *peer* is the Greek *parakupto*, translated "to stoop" in John 20:11. The thought is of one stooping down to get a closer look, to look long and hard at something. The believer is to look long and hard at **the perfect Law**, meditating on the teaching of Christ, and **remain alongside** *it*. The verb translated *remain alongside* is the Greek *parameno*. It used by Paul in Philippians 1:23 for his remaining and continuing on earth in the company of his beloved Philippians. The thought here in James is of the Christian constantly living in the company of the teaching (so the New English Bible renders it), of never leaving it, but always keeping it in mind. This man will not be simply a **hearer**, but **a doer**—an effectual **doer of** a good **work**, and therefore **will be blessed in** that **doing**. His days will be full of good works and full of the blessing of God.

It is fatally easy to **think** oneself **to be religious** and pious simply because one hears the Law or says prayers. If a man reads the Scriptures and fulfills his rule of prayer **and yet does not bridle his tongue** (compare vv. 19–20), such a man **deceives his heart**. He is *not* truly religious as he supposes; his **religion** and acts of piety are **useless** and will gain no reward from God. The **religion** that *is* **pure and undefiled before God is this: to visit orphans and widows in their tribulation, and to keep oneself unstained from the world**.

This is the piety that truly brings reward from God. One's hearing of the Word must be fulfilled in works; the hearing must result in doing (vv. 22, 25). The perfect Law of Christ's teaching counsels such acts of mercy and such commitment to holiness. The Christian must not only hear Christ's counsel, but do it.

James mentions two examples of such piety.

First he mentions the need **to visit orphans and widows** (the poorest in society and those with no recourse or help) **in their tribulation** and distress. The believer should be concerned to help the poor and to alleviate their sufferings whenever possible. For God is **the Father** to all His children, even (perhaps especially) to these humble poor.

Secondly, the believer must **keep oneself unstained from the world**. The **world** here means the network of systems and relationships that oppose God (compare 4:4)—not society as such, but worldliness. St. James here counsels not physical withdrawal from society, but inner detachment from it. This world always exerts a pull on the believer, to drag him away from fidelity to God and from poverty of spirit. True piety will cling to God's ways, showing mercy to the poor and seeking only the Kingdom.

If the believer will be a doer of the Word like this, God will reward him for such religion and piety.

ॐ ॐ ॐ ॐ ॐ

2 1 My brothers, do not have your faith of our glorious Lord Jesus Christ in partiality.

2 For if a man enters into your synagogue with gold finger-rings, in bright garb, and there also enters a poor *man* in filthy garb,

3 and you look upon the one who is wearing the bright clothes and say, "You *yourself* sit here, please," and to the poor man you say, "You *yourself* stand there, or sit by my footstool,"

4 have you not made distinctions among yourselves and become judges with evil questionings?

5 Hear, my beloved brothers: did not God choose the poor ones of the world *to be* rich in faith and heirs of the Kingdom which He has promised to those who love Him?

6 But you *yourselves* have dishonored the poor man. Do not the rich overpower you and themselves drag you into courts?

7 Do they not blaspheme the good Name which has been called over you?

8 If, indeed, you are fulfilling the royal Law, according to the Scripture, "You shall love your neighbor as yourself," you are doing well.

9 But if you show partiality, you are working sin and are exposed by the Law as transgressors.

10 For whoever keeps the whole Law and yet stumbles in one *point* has become guilty of all.

11 For He who said, "Do not commit adultery," said also, "Do not murder." Now if you do not commit adultery, but do murder, you have become a transgressor of the Law.

12 Thus speak and thus do as those about to be judged by the Law of freedom.

13 For judgment *will be* merciless to one who has not shown mercy; mercy boasts-off over judgment.

St. James then focuses upon one area where his hearers especially need to repent and become doers of the word (v. 22)—that of showing **partiality** to the rich. Such partiality to the glorious ones of this world is inconsistent with their **faith** in the **Lord Jesus Christ**, the One who is truly **glorious**, for when the Lord of glory came among us, He had nowhere to lay His head during His ministry and voluntarily washed the feet of His disciples (Matt. 8:20; John 13:1f). He thereby revealed that the true glory is that of the humble spirit, not that of outward ostentation.

Such insight, however, is far from those in the Christian assemblies. **For if a man enters into** their **synagogue** or assembly (Gr. *sunagoge*; here used for the Christian gathering itself, not the building in which it was held) **with gold finger-rings** (a sign of great wealth), dressed **in bright garb, and there also enters** at the same time **a poor *man* in filthy garb**, they **look** attentively upon the one **wearing the bright clothes**. They fawn over the rich one, saying deferentially, **"You *yourself* sit here, please"** (doubtless in a comfortable chair and in a good place), while **to the poor man** they say dismissively in the next breath, **"You *yourself* stand there, or sit by my footstool."** The poor man is either not given a seat at all, or must sit down like a slave on the floor by the footstool of someone else (lit., "*under* my footstool," sitting even lower than the footstool). When the Christians do this, can they not see that they thereby have **made distinctions among** themselves based on class, and thereby fracture their own unity? Such discrimination means that they are no better than **judges with evil questionings** or reasonings, the corrupt judges who accept bribes and try cases based on the respective wealth of those involved.

James calls them to account as his **beloved brothers**, reminding them that **God chose the poor ones of the world *to be* rich in faith**

and heirs of the Kingdom, and thereby honored the poor. It was the humble poor, the common man, upon whom Christ pronounced God's blessing and to whom He promised God's Kingdom (compare 1:9). But by their partiality, they contradict God and nullify His work by disgracing and **dishonoring the poor man** whom God would honor.

Why should they thus honor the rich? Is it not **the rich** who **overpower** them and oppress them, **and themselves** personally **drag** them **into** the **courts** of the synagogues to be flogged (compare Mark 13:9, 11)? Is it not **the rich** and unbelieving Jews who **blaspheme the good Name** of Jesus which was invoked and **called over** them in holy Baptism? The rich are the very ones who resist and oppose the Gospel. Why then fawn over such as these?

If it were the case that they were **fulfilling the royal Law** of Leviticus 19:18 (so called because it is embodied by Jesus their King), **"You shall love your neighbor as yourself,"** they would indeed be **doing well**. But when they hold the plumb line of this **Scripture** before their conduct in their assemblies, they can see that they are **showing partiality**. They are thus *not* doing well or being good Jews, but are **working sin**, and are **exposed by** this royal command of **the Law** in Leviticus 19:18 **as transgressors**.

The term *transgressors* is a strong term, equivalent to *apostates* and *renegades*. James's hearers doubtless think their conduct regarding the poor is no big deal. On the contrary, says James, that conduct proves them rebels against the Law—the worst thing a Jew could hear. For whoever would **keep the whole Law and yet stumble in** but **one** *point*, that one **has become guilty of all**.

James is not here proclaiming the necessity of sinlessness for salvation, nor speaking about involuntary sins of weakness. He is speaking about one's attitude to God, about a man who deliberately repudiates one of God's commands to defiantly choose his own way. Thus, if that man **does not commit adultery**, but **does murder**, he **has become a transgressor of the Law**, a renegade from God, for he has deliberately turned away from what God has ordered. It is no use for that man to defend himself by pointing out to God that he has not committed adultery or by showing how many of God's laws he has *not* broken. For his transgression is personal. The sin is not in breaking some abstract principle, but in rejecting a Person, for the same God **who said, "Do not commit adultery," said also, "Do not murder."** He has rejected God's authority over his life in committing the murder. In the same way, James's hearers are rejecting the God who told them to **love** their **neighbor** as themselves.

James tells them therefore to **thus speak and thus do as those about to be judged by the Law of freedom**. That is, they should speak and act as people hurrying toward the time when they will be judged by the precepts Jesus gave them (compare John 12:48; Matt. 7:24f). (These precepts are called **the Law of freedom** because when we fulfill them, we find true liberty.) In that Day, **judgment *will be* merciless to one who has not shown mercy** (such as their lack of mercy to the poor). But if they will show mercy to the poor, then on that Day, **mercy** will **boast-off over judgment**.

In saying this, James uses a vivid image, picturing mercy and condemnatory judgment as two adversaries. Which will prove the stronger? If we follow Christ's Law of freedom and show mercy to the poor, then mercy will triumph on the Last Day. The verb rendered *boast-off* is the Greek *katakauxaomai*, an intensive of the verb with *kauxaomai*, to boast. It is used in Romans 11:18 and means "to exult," "to crow." The image here is of mercy exultantly shouting in triumph over a defeated judgment, to our eternal salvation. Yet mercy will only triumph on the Day if we refuse to show partiality, and strive to love all men as Christ commanded.

🙙 🙙 🙙 🙙 🙙

14 What *is* the profit, my brothers, if a man says he has faith but does not have works? Is the faith able to save him?

15 If a brother or sister exists naked and lacks daily food,

16 and anyone of you says to them, "Go in peace, be warmed and fed *to the full*," yet you do not give them the things needful for the body, what *is* the profit *of that*?

31

> 17 Thus faith, if it does not have works, is dead, *being* by itself.
>
> 18 But someone will say, "You *yourself* have faith, and I *myself* have works: show me your faith without the works, and I *myself* will show you *my* faith from my works."
>
> 19 You *yourselves* have faith that God is one. You do well; even the demons have faith—and shudder.

For if one's life is devoid of works and consumed by such sins as partiality, **what profit** will he gain on the Last Day from that? As a Jew, no doubt he would **say** that **he has faith**, believing in the one true God. But if he does not have works, is that **faith able to save him?** Suppose, James says, a **brother or sister exists naked**, going about in rags or without an outer garment to stay warm, and **lacks** even **daily food**. (The inclusion of **sister** with **brother** is unusual and perhaps points to the widows.) And suppose that **anyone** of them **says to them, "Go in peace, be warmed and fed *to the full*"** and then goes off, yet **does not give them the things needful for the body**. How comically ridiculous is such a charade! **What *is* the profit** of *that* on the Last Day? Obviously, then, merely having a cerebral faith in God and His Christ is not able to save, for such **faith, if it does not have works, is dead, *being* by itself**.

Some in the Christian community may claim to be safe at the Judgment because they have faith. To such a person, it is enough to refute him for **someone** to say, **"You *yourself* have faith, and I *myself* have works: show me your faith without the works, and I *myself* will show you *my* faith from my works"** (the pronouns are emphatic, to stress the contrast). That is, confession of faith may stand alone, without any works, but truly Christian works spring from saving faith and presuppose it. Thus, *works are the only way in which truly saving faith can be shown to exist.* The complacent brother may think he is safe because he **has faith that God is one**. As a good Jew, he confesses to all the world the unity of God and is a monotheist. He **does well**, for God is indeed the only One, and his confession is true. But **even the demons** could make this confession and **have faith** that God is one—and they **shudder** at the thought. Obviously more is required than simple head faith.

> ࿓ ࿓ ࿓ ࿓ ࿓
>
> 20 But are you willing to know, you empty man, that the faith without the works is idle?
>
> 21 Was not Abraham our father justified from works when he offered up Isaac his son upon the altar?
>
> 22 You see that the faith was co-working with his works, and from the works, faith was perfected,
>
> 23 and the Scripture was fulfilled which says, "Abraham had faith in God, and it was reckoned to him for righteousness," and he was called the Friend of God.
>
> 24 You see that a man is justified from works, and not from faith alone.
>
> 25 Likewise was not Rahab the prostitute also justified from works when she welcomed the messengers and sent them out by a different way?
>
> 26 For just as the body without the spirit is dead, thus also the faith without works is dead.

James then challenges his adversary directly, denouncing him as an **empty man** for his refusal to repent and strive for good works. The words *empty man* (Gr. *anthrope kene*) are meant to goad James's unrepentant hearer, spurring him to repentance and action. How could you, James asks, be such a blockhead as not to know that **the faith without the works is idle** and useless? (A play on words lurks in the Greek: "faith without works [Gr. *ergon*] is idle [Gr. *arge*—lit., "without work"].) For anyone could know this simply by recalling the example of **Abraham our father**.

They can see from the story in Genesis 22 that the great

patriarch was **justified from works**. It was not enough that he had faith that God existed. That **faith was perfected** and became real in his life only when he obeyed God and **offered up Isaac his son upon the altar**. It was only when **faith was co-working with his works** that **the Scripture was fulfilled which says, "Abraham had faith in God, and it was reckoned to him for righteousness," and he was called the Friend of God.** If Abraham had refused to offer up Isaac and had not done that work, he would not have enjoyed the righteousness and blessing of being the Friend and colleague of God.

The phrase *faith was co-working with his works* (Gr. *pistis sunergei tois ergois autou*) means that faith is inseparable from works. It is **from works** that **faith** is **perfected**, fulfilled, realized and made real. Thus **a man is justified from works, and not from faith alone**, for faith is only truly faith when it produces works.

The proof that faith is only made real through works is proved even more conclusively by the case of **Rahab**, whose story is told in Joshua 2. One might object that Abraham is the exception, that he was saved by works because he was a man of exceptional righteousness. But James adduces also the example of the pagan Rahab, one who was not a pillar of righteousness, but a **prostitute**. She also was **justified from works when she welcomed the** Jewish **messengers** who were spying out the land **and sent them out by a different way** from the one by which they came, thus saving their lives. (The verb rendered *sent out* is actually better rendered "cast out," Gr. *ekballo*, for she sent them out in haste to flee back to their Israelite camp.)

Rahab came to believe in the Jewish God, who was giving Israel victory over the peoples of Canaan. But simply believing in the Jewish God was not enough. Rather, she had to express her new loyalty and faith in the concrete act of hiding the spies from their pursuers and sending them home safely. It was only thus that she saved herself and her family and won a place among the Chosen People after the fall of Jericho (see Joshua 6:25). Her new faith in the Jewish God was thus realized through her work of hiding the Jewish spies.

From the diverse examples of Abraham and Rahab, it is apparent that **just as the body without the spirit is dead, thus also the faith without works is dead**. One can have **body without** breath or animating **spirit**, but such is a mere corpse, of no use to anyone. In the same way, **faith without works** is not real faith, but is equally **dead** and useless. Faith needs works to be alive, just as the body needs the animating spirit.

❧ EXCURSUS:
ON FAITH AND WORKS IN JAMES AND PAUL

The perceived tension between James and Paul on the subject of faith and works is one which has vexed theologians. Some have suggested that Paul and James are speaking in conscious opposition to each other, or at the very least that their teachings are antithetical.

This, however, is not the case. James was writing before Paul began his literary work, so James was obviously not writing in contradiction of Paul. Nor, in fact, was Paul writing in contradiction of James. Both addressed separate issues and confronted different (and opposite) errors.

When Paul wrote that a man is saved by faith, not by works (e.g. Rom. 3:28; Gal. 2:16), he was striving against those Jews who said that merely being an obedient disciple of Jesus was not enough to be saved. One also needed, they insisted, to earn God's favor by performing works of the Law (the first of which, for the Gentile, was circumcision). This was the spirit of the Pharisees, the proud determination to earn salvation by one's own efforts. These Jews said that a Gentile could not be truly forgiven and saved as he was, but that he needed to become a circumcised Jew first. For Paul, such an attitude indicated a complete failure to understand the Gospel, and involved subverting everything to make Christ's saving Cross subordinate to the Law.

When James wrote that a man is saved by works and not by faith alone (2:24), he was striving against those Jewish Christians who felt that to be saved it was sufficient simply to confess the faith, and that the quality of one's life was irrelevant. For these people, a merely nominal and cerebral

---

faith was all that was needed, and it did not matter that their supposed discipleship to Jesus was not at all manifested in their daily lives. For James, such an attitude indicated a complete failure to understand the Gospel, and those who clung to such an attitude were no true disciples of Jesus at all.

For James, as for Paul, what saves a man is heartfelt discipleship to Christ. One is saved by faith, faithfulness (both English words translated by the Gr. *pistis*), a relationship of humble love for God. This relationship begins when one receives forgiveness as a free gift through Christ and is sustained by a life of repentant striving to please God. Both James and Paul knew that a love for God that is not reflected in love for man is an illusion.

James found this truth under attack by nominalists who said that a life of striving to please God was not necessary, as long as one gave intellectual assent to certain doctrinal truths (such as the unity of God). He therefore insisted that one is saved by works, so that one's inner faith is shown to be authentic by the quality of one's life. Paul found this truth under attack by legalists who said that this life was not received as a free gift, but needed to be earned by piling up good works. He therefore insisted that one is saved by faith, by receiving forgiveness freely as one comes to God in Christ. Neither apostle contradicted the other, but each protected the same Gospel from different foes and distortions.

§IV.   Exhortation to the Meekness of Wisdom (3:1—4:12)

ᘒ ᘒ ᘒ ᘒ ᘒ

3 1 **Let not many become teachers, my brothers, knowing that we will receive more judgment.**

James now exhorts his hearers to meekness. Many among them tended to arrogance, and some coveted the teaching office, thinking that becoming a teacher in the Church would make them more prominent. Their desire to become teachers was thus not motivated by a love of wisdom and a desire to spread it. Rather, it was motivated by a love of status and a desire to dominate.

The office of teacher (Gr. *didaskalos*) was a common one (see Acts 13:1; Eph. 4:11). Teaching, along with ruling, was one of the tasks of the elders or presbyters, and elders who labored hard at it were accounted worthy of double honor (see 1 Tim. 5:17). (The offices of teacher and presbyter in fact tended to coalesce; Paul refers to both shepherds and teachers in the same breath in Eph. 4:11, probably because both roles were often filled by the same man.) Especially in a Jewish context, with its cultural respect for teaching rabbis, the office of teacher was a prestigious one, and it is not surprising that those who loved the praise of man gravitated to it.

St. James, however, warns against **many becoming teachers**, knowing that a number of the aspirants are motivated by desire for status. He therefore warns them off, reminding them that teachers like himself (he is a part of the **we**) **will receive more judgment**. The words rendered *more judgment* (Gr. *meizon krima*) could also be rendered "stricter judgment," or even, "more condemnation." (The word *krima* often has an unfavorable connotation; compare its use in Rom. 3:8; 5:16; 2 Pet. 2:3; Jude 4; Rev. 17:1.) Teachers' words affect many, and so if their teaching misleads, many others suffer harm. That is the reason they will incur **more judgment** on the Last Day.

ॐ ॐ ॐ ॐ ॐ

2 For all trip in many ways. If anyone does not trip in word, this one *is* a perfect man, able to bridle the whole body also.

3 Now if we put the bits into the horses' mouths so as to make them obey us, we guide their whole body also.

4 Behold, the ships also, being so great and driven by hard winds, are guided by a very small

rudder, wherever the impulse of the one steering intends.

5 Thus also the tongue is a little part of the body, and it boasts of great *things*. Behold, a small fire kindles how great a wood!

6 And the tongue *is* a fire, the world of unrighteousness; the tongue is set among our members as that which stains the whole body, and sets aflame the wheel of birth, and is set aflame by Gehenna.

7 For every species of beasts and birds, both of reptiles and sea creatures, is subdued and has been subdued by the human species.

8 But no one is able to subdue the human tongue—a restless wickedness, full of death-bearing poison.

9 With it we bless the Lord and Father; and with it we curse the men, who have been made according to the likeness of God;

10 from the same mouth come out blessing and cursing. My brothers, these things ought not to be thus!

11 Does a fountain pour forth from the same hole the sweet and the bitter?

12 Is a fig tree, my brothers, able to make olives, or a vine *able to make* figs? Neither can salt water make sweet.

In continuing his warning against arrogance and dissuading his hearers from becoming teachers, James points out that the teacher depends upon the spoken **word**. This, he says, shows how dangerous the teaching office can be, **for all** people **trip in many ways**, and the one who **does not trip** in what he says is **a perfect man, able to bridle** not just his tongue, but his **whole body also**. That is, in our fallen state, we are all prone to sin, and particularly with the tongue. The tongue is, in fact, usually the last member to be tamed. Sins of speech—such as gossip, slander, verbal abuse, haughty or angry speech—are especially hard to eradicate. Success in this is usually a sign of having become **perfect**, spiritually mature (Gr. *teleios*). Control of the tongue is pivotal, for that little member is responsible for much damage. As the Scripture says, "Many have fallen by the edge of the sword, but not so many as have fallen because of the tongue" (Sir. 28:18).

Some may think this a somewhat exaggerated claim, but James supports it with examples which show that a small thing can have big effects. If we can put **the bits into the horses' mouths**, we can **make them obey us** and **guide their whole body also**, even though the horse is much larger and more powerful than a man. Thus, a bit, though little, can have a great effect. The same principle is seen in **ships also**. Though ships are **so great and driven by hard winds** so as to be apparently unstoppable, they can be **guided by a very small rudder**, so that the whole huge ship goes **wherever the impulse of the one steering intends**. Again we see what great results can come from something small. It is **thus** with the tongue: though it **is a little part of the body**, it **boasts of great *things***, being able to inflict untold damage. Anyone can see this, for all know how a camp **fire**, though **small**, can still **kindle** a **great wood** and set all the forest ablaze.

In fact, St. James continues, the image is apt, for **the tongue *is* a fire**, spreading destruction all around. It is a complete **world of unrighteousness**, containing within itself all the vast potentialities for sin and having a crucial role to play in all the evil in the world. In our fallen state, **the tongue is set among our members as that which stains** and defiles **the whole body**. That is, when we consider our bodily life, we see that the tongue is the member responsible for our ruin. Indeed, it **sets aflame the wheel of birth**, and **is** itself **set aflame by Gehenna**.

The phrase *wheel of birth* (Gr. *troxon tes geneseos*), though used in Greek philosophical writings to indicate reincarnation, in the mouth of a Jew like James has a more homely meaning. It refers here to the varying fortunes of our days, beginning from the day of our birth, the whole revolving cycle of seasons that makes up our life.

The tongue, James says, **sets aflame** all our days and months and years, burning and consuming them. And not surprisingly, since it itself **is set aflame by Gehenna**. The fire that burns in **Gehenna**, or hell, is that which kindles the fire of the tongue. That is, just as the fire of Gehenna burns with uncontrollable fury, so the fire spread by the tongue will burn with uncontrollable fury, consuming everything before it.

The tongue, therefore, is untamable, worse than any wild beast. For **every species has been subdued by the human species**—both species **of beasts and** also of **birds** (which are harder to tame, since they fly beyond our reach), both species **of reptiles and** also of **sea creatures** (harder to tame, since they live in the sea). The human species has subdued and tamed them all. But for all his power to subdue all of nature around him, **no one is able to subdue the human tongue**. The tongue of this human species remains untamed and untamable. It is **a restless wickedness**. The word translated *restless* is the Greek *akatastatos*. It means "unsettled," "unstable," and its cognate *akatastasia* is used in Luke 21:9 to describe the tumults which, along with wars, afflict the world. The tongue, therefore, is always in a state of tumult, its evil ever ready to break out; it is **full of death-bearing poison**, able to kill any relationship.

James reminds us of how unnatural the tongue is. For with the same tongue **we bless the Lord and Father** (a pious Jew pronounced the Eighteen Benedictions every day, blessing God over and again for His mercies), and we also **curse the men** we encounter, even though these **have been made according to the likeness of God**. If men are made in God's image, should we not then bless them, even as we bless God? **From the same mouth come out** both **blessing and cursing**. This is like a freak of nature and **ought not to be thus**.

For where else in all creation could we find such a monstrosity, something which is the source of two opposites? **Does a fountain pour forth from the same hole** both **the sweet** and fresh water, and also **the bitter** and brackish water? No; the fountain pours forth either good water or bad, but not both. Or consider the trees: **is a fig tree able to make olives, or a vine *able to make* figs?** No;

each tree produces but one fruit, and there is always consistency. Or consider the lakes: either a lake is **salt water** or **sweet** (that is, fresh) water. But the saltwater lake will not one day produce fresh water. In all nature—in fountains, trees, lakes—one sees reliability. It is only the tongue that is unnatural, one day producing blessing and the next day cursing.

ॐ ॐ ॐ ॐ ॐ

13 Who among you *is* wise and understanding? Let him show by his good conduct his works in the meekness of wisdom.

14 But if you have bitter jealousy and opportunism in your heart, do not boast-off and lie against the truth.

15 This wisdom is not that which comes down from above, but is earthly, soulish, demonic.

16 For where jealousy and opportunism *are*, there *is* tumult and every base practice.

17 But the wisdom from above is first pure, then peaceful, forbearing, compliant, full of mercy and good fruits, unwavering, unhypocritical.

18 And the fruit of righteousness is sown in peace by those who make peace.

What this extended denunciation of the sins of the tongue leads to is this: anyone among them claiming to be **wise and understanding** (and perhaps aspiring to be teachers) must **show by his good conduct his works in the meekness of wisdom**. True **wisdom**, therefore, is shown by **meekness**, not arrogance. But **if** they **have bitter jealousy and opportunism in** their **heart** instead of meekness, let them not dare to approach the teaching office, for then they will not please God or further His work. Rather, their work will simply be **boasting-off** and crowing (Gr. *katakauxomai*; compare 2:13). Instead of teaching **the truth**, they will be **lying against** it by the quality of their life as they use their authority to dominate others. Sadly, one can preach and speak with such arrogance that a thoughtful listener will conclude the preaching cannot be true, and the Name of God can be blasphemed among the Gentiles because of us (Rom. 2:24).

The so-called **wisdom** such men impart is **not** the true wisdom **which comes down from** God **above**. Rather, it is the false wisdom, that which is merely **earthly, soulish, demonic**. The teaching ministries of such arrogant men do not savor of heaven or lead people closer to God. Their so-called wisdom is **earthly** and earthbound, a mere rehash of secular ideas. It is **soulish** (Gr. *psuchikos*, related to *psuche*, the soul), that is, characterized by life in this sense-oriented age, sensual. It is **demonic**, open to influence by the demons, who oppose the work of God. If these men become teachers and exercise leadership motivated by **jealousy and opportunism**, by the ambitious desire to overcome a rival (compare v. 14), the result in the Church will be **tumult** and disturbance (Gr. *akatastasia*; compare the cognate adjective in v. 8), accompanied by **every base practice**. How many conflicts in congregations are caused by this! What catastrophe unbending arrogance brings!

However, the true **wisdom**, that which is **from** God **above** and comes down as His gift, is very different. It is **first** of all **pure** (Gr. *agnos*). Above all, it is unmixed with baser desires for self-gratification (especially regarding sexuality), and free from all self-promotion, for the true teacher thinks only of helping his flock, not of exalting himself. The true wisdom may also be recognized by being **peaceful, forbearing, compliant, full of mercy and good fruits, unwavering, unhypocritical.**

In piling up these adjectives, St. James shows that one may recognize the truly divine wisdom by the willingness not to insist on one's own way. The truly wise teacher is **peaceful** (Gr. *eirenikos*), not quarrelsome. He is **forbearing**, gentle, yielding (Gr. *epieikes*), and does not insist on the letter of the law. He is **compliant** (Gr. *eupeithes*), ready to be persuaded by someone else of a different point of view. He is **full of mercy**, eager to forgive, like the Lord. He is also **unwavering** (Gr. *adiakritos*; compare *diakrino* in 1:6), sticking to the truth with no regard for personal favoritism. He is **unhypocritical** and genuine, not currying favor with the rich. The **fruit of**

righteousness and maturity in the lives of the faithful (by which one can recognize the true teacher) **is sown in peace by those who make peace.** That is, the true teacher is a man of peace, teaching in a spirit of peace, and always willing to conciliate and make peace. If a man is overbearing and quarrelsome and always insists on his own way, it is certain that he does not have the wisdom that comes down from above.

ॐ ॐ ॐ ॐ ॐ

4 1   From where *are the* wars and from where *the* quarrels among you? Are they not from your pleasures soldiering in your members?

2   You desire and do not have, *so* you murder; and you are jealous and are not able to attain *what you want*, *so* you quarrel and war. You do not have because you do not ask.

3   You ask and do not receive, because you ask wickedly, that you may spend *it* on your pleasures.

4   You adulteresses! Do you not know that the friendship with the world is enmity with God? Therefore whoever intends to be a friend of the world appoints himself an enemy of God.

5   Or do you think that the Scripture says vainly about envy, "He longs for the spirit He made to dwell in us"?*

6   But He gives more grace. Therefore it says, "God opposes the arrogant, but gives grace to the humble."

7   Submit therefore to God. Withstand the devil and he will flee from you.

8   Draw near to God and He will draw near to you. Cleanse your hands, you sinners,

---

* I am indebted to Prof. Albert Pietersma for help with this translation of the Greek of v. 5.

> and purify your hearts, you double-souled!
> 9 Be miserable and mourn and weep; let your laughter be turned into mourning, and your joy to dejection.
> 10 Be humbled before the Lord, and He will exalt you.
> 11 Do not speak against one another, brothers. The one speaking against a brother or judging his brother speaks against the Law and judges the Law; but if you judge the Law, you are not a doer of the Law, but a judge.
> 12 There is one Lawgiver and Judge, the One who is able to save and to destroy. But who are you, the one judging your neighbor?

The chapter break notwithstanding, James continues his previous exhortation to meekness and peace, next taking aim at the longstanding feuds (the **wars**) and the outbreaking conflicts (the **quarrels**) that characterize some of his hearers. James pinpoints their source: the **pleasures** and passions **soldiering in** their **members** and bodies. The word rendered *soldiering* is the Greek *strateuo*, cognate with the word *stratiotes*, "soldier." The image is of the passions waging war in the bodies of his hearers, and taking over more and more of their lives.

Speaking like a prophet of old, St. James denounces those whose lives are given up to pursuit of pleasure: **You desire and do not have, so you murder; and you are jealous and are not able to attain *what you want*, so you quarrel and war**. Some commentators find the reference to murder too jarring and try to deflect its force, either by suggesting that James means simply hating enough to murder (see 1 John 3:15), or by changing the verb *phoneuete* ("to murder") to read *phthoneite* ("to envy").

I would suggest that neither of these expedients is necessary. James is addressing Christians who are merely nominal and who are wealthy landowners (perhaps those rich ones referred to in 2:2).

They are not, of course, deliberately murdering people. But in their escalating **desire** to **have** more and more, some are unjustly withholding the wages of those who work their lands (5:4), so that the impoverished laborers are dying, weakened by malnourishment and subject to disease. Thus the landowners unwittingly **murder** the laborers in their never-satisfied lust to grow ever richer (5:6). It is this **jealous** coveting and desire for wealth that causes them to **quarrel** and **war** with their rich neighbors.

Given this greed and quarreling, all their piety is in vain. It seems that the rich are asking for God's help in their quest for wealth, but meeting setback after setback (see Haggai 1:9–11). The famine that hit Palestine in the years immediately prior may be relevant here: if James wrote this epistle in AD 48, the effects of the famine (which began in about the year 44) would still be present. It is possible that the rich are asking for divine relief from the effects of this famine. (The recent famine would also explain the deaths of laborers.) James says that the rich **do not have** the requested help because they **do not ask** God. That is, their prayers do not reach heaven because they **ask wickedly, that** they **may spend** the requested wealth on their **pleasures**—and not on the suffering poor who labor for them. They **do not receive** any help from God because all their prayers are offered from selfish motives, and from a heart in the grip of jealousy and greed, of hatred and judgmentalism.

James rounds on these so-called Christians like a prophet of old, calling them **adulteresses** (see Is. 54:5; Jer. 3:20; Ezek. 16:32). Believers are in covenant to God even as a wife is to her husband, but these have abandoned fidelity to God and have gone running off after Mammon. Such intimate **friendship with the world**, such prostration before the world's values, **is enmity with God**. Do they **not know** something as basic as this? They must therefore choose whom they will serve (see Matt. 6:24)—either God or the world. For **whoever intends to be a friend of the world appoints himself an enemy of God**. They may imagine that they are still God's friends, as Abraham was (James 2:23), and are just trying to get ahead. James utterly rejects such rationalization. Their greed and worldliness mean that they have abandoned God and are now

His self-appointed foes. And they know only too well what doom lies in store for God's foes.

James turns to **the Scripture** for confirmation of his condemnation of the **envy** that motivates them. Quoting a conflation of such passages as Genesis 2:7; Isaiah 63:11; Zechariah 1:14; 12:1, James reminds them that God **longs for the spirit He made to dwell in** them. That is, human envy and pursuit of worldly wealth make us God's enemies because He **longs** for our inner devotion and will brook no rivals.

But God **gives more grace**, more than enough to conquer the sin of envy. **Therefore it says** in Proverbs 3:34, **"God opposes the arrogant, but gives grace to the humble."** They must therefore become the **humble** who receive God's grace; they must **submit therefore to God** and return to Him. Let them **withstand the devil**, who incites them to envy and greed; **he will** surely **flee from** them if they do. The way back to life stands open. If they will but **draw near to God** in repentance, **He will draw near** to them in return, for He longs for them (v. 5). Though they consider themselves faithful, they are in reality **sinners** and apostates, **double-souled** men who confess faith in God while they serve the world (Gr. *dipsuchos*; compare 1:8). Their hands drip with the blood of those who have died (Isaiah 1:15); let them now **cleanse** their **hands** and **purify** their greedy **hearts** by a determination to help the poor, so that both their outer actions and their inner motivations will show their faith.

Now is the time for repentance and for fasting (see also Joel 1:14f, which was also occasioned by a famine). Let the rich now **be miserable and mourn and weep** for their sins. **Let** the **laughter** of their unrighteous feasting **be turned into mourning**, let their selfish **joy** be turned to **dejection** as they fast and consider their sins. If they will thus **be humbled before the Lord, He will exalt** them. He will forgive and restore them.

James concludes his exhortation to meekness with a final appeal: let them **not speak against one another**. In the past, they cursed and reviled their neighbor in their feuding and quarreling. But no more. For **the one speaking against a brother or judging his brother** in reality thereby **speaks against the Law and judges the**

Law—an unthinkable thing for a Jew. The Law commands us to love our neighbor (Lev. 19:18), and to condemn our brother is to condemn the Law, since we are thereby defying its commandment. Anyone who would presume to judge and condemn the Law is manifestly **not a doer of the Law** (as all Jews strove to be). Instead, this one is **a judge**. And that is to usurp God's role, for He alone is the **one Lawgiver and Judge**—the only **One who is able to save and to destroy**. Do they imagine that the power of life and death is with them? Then let God be Judge alone, and let them refrain from judging their brothers. For who are they to think they can usurp God's role?

§V.   Exhortation to Humble Contentment (4:13–17)

ॐ ॐ ॐ ॐ ॐ

13 Come now, you who say, "Today or tomorrow we will go into this or that city, and do *business for* a year there and trade and *make a* profit."

14 You do not understand what your life *will be* tomorrow. You are a vapor that appears for a little *while* and then disappears.

15 Instead, you *ought* to say, "If the Lord wills, we will live and also do this or that."

16 But now you boast in your pretensions; all such boasting is evil.

17 Therefore, to one who knows the good thing to do, and not doing *it*, to him it is sin.

James now begins another exhortation, urging his hearers to be content and to humbly submit to God, whatever their lot. He begins by saying, **Come now**, challenging his hearers to defend themselves. In particular, he addresses those **who say, "Today or tomorrow we will go into this or that city, and do *business for* a year there and trade and *make a* profit."** Once again, the rich are addressed, and St. James takes aim at their **pretensions** and their pride. These ones proudly assume they have power over their own lives. They **do not understand** and cannot guess **what** their **life *will be* tomorrow**. Tomorrow they may or may not be able to go into this or that city, and if they do, they may not live to spend a day there, much less a year. Nor do they know, if God does spare them to live a year, whether they will make a profit or endure a loss. They assume their own power, but in reality they are but **a vapor**, something that **appears for a little *while* and then disappears**. Human life vanishes as quickly as the morning mist, and we can therefore not presume on our permanency.

Instead of such self-confidence, they ***ought* to say, "If the Lord wills, we will live and also do this or that."** They may plan freely, but in humility must confess that all human planning is contingent and utterly dependent on the will of God. Perhaps we will live through the night, or perhaps not. If we live, perhaps we will fulfill our plan, or perhaps not. All is in the hand of God. Refusal to acknowledge this shows our **pretensions**, our vain boasting. It is not a sign of commendable energy, of our being a "real go-getter," but of **evil**. Now that James has brought to their attention their presumption, to refuse humility is **sin**, pure and simple. Sins of omission bring God's judgment, just as do sins of commission.

§VI.   Exhortation to Be Patient under Suffering (5:1–11)

℈ ℈ ℈ ℈ ℈

5 1   Come now, you rich, weep and howl for your miseries that are coming upon you.

2   Your riches have rotted and your garments have become moth-eaten.

3   Your gold and your silver have corroded; and their rust will be a witness against you and will eat your flesh as fire. It is in the last days that you have treasured up.

4   Behold, the reward of the workers who have mown your fields, which has been withheld by you, cries out, and the shouts of those who

> harvested have entered into the ears of the Lord of Sabaoth!
>
> 5 You have *lived* indulgently upon the earth and *reveled in* luxury; you have nourished your hearts in a day of slaughter.
>
> 6 You have sentenced *as guilty* and murdered the righteous *man*; he does not withstand you.

In this denunciation James addresses the resolutely impenitent rich who oppress their poor Jewish Christian workers. **The reward and wage of those workers**, the ones **who have mown** their **fields, has been withheld** by them, so that the poor starved during the recent famine and died in their poverty (see comments on 4:2). It is as if the rich **sentenced** them *as guilty* and **murdered the righteous** themselves. Certainly the poor and powerless worker did **not withstand** them, because he was not able to do so.

Like a prophet of old, James pronounces the doom of God upon such impenitent oppressors. The money owing **cries out** to God, like the blood of Abel (Gen. 4:10), and the workers' **shouts** to God for justice, though they seemed to go unheard, **have entered into the ears of the Lord of Sabaoth**, the Lord of Hosts, the Commander of heavenly armies, He who is strong to avenge His people. (The use of the term *Lord of Sabaoth* places this squarely within the prophetic tradition in which God executes justice on the earth; compare for example Is. 2:12.)

The rich have stored up immense wealth through their oppression of their workers, treasuring up **riches** of grain, and **garments** (a source of wealth in those days), and **gold** and **silver**. On the day of judgment, they will find their produce has **rotted**, their garments have **become moth-eaten**, and even their **gold** (which cannot corrode) and their **silver** have supernaturally **corroded**. The fact that these have been stored up and left to rot (and thus not used to help the poor to whom they were owed) will **be a witness against** them. Let them **weep and howl for** the **miseries that** will be **coming upon** them at that Judgment. Such unjust wealth will **eat** their **flesh as fire**, fueling the flames of Gehenna.

The rich think they will live forever and justice will never find them out. But it is **in the last days** that they **treasure up** their wealth. They should have known the Day of Judgment was fast approaching and used their wealth to help the poor. They use their riches to *live* **indulgently upon the earth and** *revel in* **luxury**. They **nourish** and fatten their **hearts** with their constant feasting and their excess. They do not know they are like the calves that are only being fattened for the **day of slaughter**.

❧ ❧ ❧ ❧ ❧

7   Be patient, therefore, brothers, until the Coming of the Lord. Behold, the farmer waits for the precious fruit of the earth, being patient for it, until it receives the early and late *rains*.

8   You *yourselves* also be patient; establish your hearts, for the Coming of the Lord draws near!

9   Do not groan, brothers, against one another, lest you be judged. Behold, the Judge is standing before the doors!

10 As an example, brothers, of suffering hardship and of patience, take the prophets who spoke in the Name of the Lord.

11 Behold, we *count* blessed those who persevered. You have heard of the perseverance of Job, and have seen the end *purpose* of the Lord, that the Lord is full of heartfelt *love* and is compassionate.

James then turns to address his **brothers** with tenderness and compassion. Those who are suffering under the oppression of the rich should **be patient**. Zealots in Israel at that time were tempted to take matters into their own hands and violently overthrow the oppressors themselves. James once and for all closes this door. They must wait **until the Coming of the Lord**. As farming workers, they know this. They know how **the farmer waits for the precious**

fruit of the earth, being patient for it, until it receives the early and late *rains*, in the fall and spring. It is only after these rains that harvesting can begin. Attempts to harvest early result in no fruit. In the same way, they must **also be patient** and not imagine that justice will come if they attempt to harvest early by violence or revolution. They must therefore **establish** their **hearts** and refuse to be shaken from their serene stability in Christ. His **Coming draws near**. He will come soon enough.

As they wait, they are **not** to **groan** and complain **against one another**. During times of persecution, there is always the temptation to quarrel and to break into factions (see Phil. 1:27–28), even as fearful animals have a tendency to snap and bite. If the Christians condemn and judge one another, they themselves will **be judged** (Matt. 7:1). Let them refuse to judge before the time. **Behold, the** true **Judge is standing before the doors**, ready to enter! Let them wait for Him. He will do all the judging necessary.

As an inspiring **example of suffering hardship and of patience**, let them **take the prophets who spoke in the Name of the Lord**. Let them remember the struggles of Elijah, whose life was persecuted by his king (1 Kg. 19). Let them remember the sufferings of Jeremiah, who was beaten, imprisoned, cast into an empty cistern, and left to die (Jer. 19; 37—38). Let them remember the martyrdom of Isaiah, who was sawn in half (Heb. 11:37). Despite their sufferings, we now *count* them **blessed who persevered** through such things. We too therefore will be blessed on the Last Day if we persevere as they did. And all **have heard of the perseverance of Job, and have seen the end** *purpose* **of the Lord** in His dealings with him (Job 42). When Job had endured all his sufferings, refusing to abandon God, the Lord restored him to joy, for He **is full of heartfelt** *love* **and is compassionate**.

The word rendered *full of heartfelt love* is the Greek *polusplagchnos*, derived from *polu* ("many") and *splagchna* (lit. "innards"). The innards were spoken of as the seat of emotion; thus, to love from the *splagchna* is to love from one's deepest heart, with an abundant overflowing love. St. James says here that God's heart overflows with love for us, that He longs to be **compassionate** and merciful, to wipe away our tears and fill us with joy. Let us persevere and hold to our faith, waiting for the Lord to bless us in the age to come, even as He blessed Job after his sufferings were over.

§VII.   Exhortation to Avoid Oaths (5:12)

> ❧ ❧ ❧ ❧ ❧
>
> 12 But before all *things*, my brothers, do not swear, either by the heaven or by the earth or with any other oath; but let your yes be yes, and *your* no, no, lest you fall under judgment.

James next exhorts his brothers to **not swear, either by the heaven or by the earth or with any other oath**. God will indeed bless them at the end in His overflowing compassion, but only if they take care in the meantime not to swear rashly.

Casual oaths were part of the everyday language of the Palestinian Jew, and the Pharisees had a series of gradations by which some oaths were considered as not binding (for example, swearing by the Temple), and other oaths as binding (such as swearing by the gold of the Temple; see Matt. 23:16). The result of such legalistic casuistry was to devalue the spoken word and make rash vows very common.

For James, as for his Lord (see Matt. 5:34–37), the Christian should **not swear** at all, but be so truthful that his **yes** means **yes** and his **no** means **no**, so that no other oaths are necessary. Otherwise, God will hold him accountable for oaths rashly sworn, and he will **fall under judgment**. The compassion and blessing promised in verse 13 can only be gained if the Christians do not invite God's judgment with their tongues.

In our culture, we are not given to making hasty oaths and promises to God. We are, however, given to a casual use of the divine Name, and James's counsel here rebukes that also. The Name of God and Jesus Christ should be pronounced by Christians only with reverent love.

§VIII. Exhortation to Prayer (5:13–18)

ॐ ॐ ॐ ॐ ॐ

13 *If* anyone among you is suffering hardship, let him pray. *If* anyone is cheerful, let him sing.

14 *If* anyone is ailing, let him call for the elders of the church and let them pray over him, anointing him with oil in the Name of the Lord.

15 And the prayer of the faith will save the one who is wasting away, and the Lord will raise him up, and if he has done sins, it will be forgiven him.

16 Therefore confess *your* sins to one another and pray for one another that you may be cured. The working supplication of a righteous man has much strength.

17 Elijah was a man of like-nature to us, and he prayed with prayer that it might not rain, and it did not rain upon the earth for three years and six months.

18 And he prayed again, and the heaven gave rain, and the earth sprouted its fruit.

Next St. James urges his hearers to find their center and contentment in God, whatever their varied circumstances of life. If **anyone is suffering hardship, let him pray**, offering his suffering to God. The hardship referred to is mainly that of suffering persecution (the Greek verb is *kakopatheo*, the same word used in v. 10 to describe the sufferings of the prophets), but here includes any form of suffering. And one should not pray to God to remove the hardship, but for strength to endure it and use it for good, to purify the heart.

If **anyone is cheerful** and light of heart, **let him sing**, thanking God for the blessings that cheer him. James does not direct what to sing, but it is likely that he has the praises of the Psalter in mind; the verb rendered *sing* is the Greek *psallo*, cognate with *psalmos*, "psalm."

Daily blessings ought not to be taken for granted, but should be acknowledged as gifts from God and should anchor us in Him.

If **anyone is ailing, let him call for the elders** [Gr. *presbuteros*] **of the church**, so that the elders may **pray over him, anointing him with oil in the Name of the Lord**. James promises that **the prayer of the faith** (that is, the prayer offered in faith) **will save the one who is wasting away, and the Lord will raise him up** from his sickbed, **and if he has done sins, it will be forgiven him**.

In St. James's day, the one who was very ill (**wasting away**, Gr. *kamno*; used for the fatigued, but also for the dying; see Wisdom 15:9) would call for all the presbyters in the city, and they would gather around him to pray. They would **anoint** the sick person **with oil**, invoking **the Name of the Lord** Jesus over him and praying for his healing (compare Mark 6:13). The presbyters thus represented the totality of the Christian community, united in intercession for one of their sick. The sick one would of course pray also, confessing his sins and asking God's mercy. **If he has done sins** (it is not stated as a certainty), **it will be forgiven him**, for the healing from God would come upon his soul as well as his body. This practice continues in the Church today as the Sacrament of Oil or Unction, though in most Orthodox parishes, only one presbyter, the pastor, is able to do the anointing.

Because of the Lord's willingness to heal, James urges his hearers to **confess** their **sins to one another and pray for one another, that** they **may be cured**. This confession is not to be confused with today's regular sacramental confession and absolution (which in the days of the early Church was mostly confined to reconciling the penitent who had been excommunicated from the Church). What James has in mind is the sick man openly confessing his sins to God before those who have come to pray for him. (James speaks of confessing sins **to one another**, for sickness may strike any, and the one who today prays for the sick and hears his confession may tomorrow become sick and make a confession.)

Such confession was commonplace in the early Church. An early church manual, dating from around AD 100 and called the *Didache* (or "Teaching"), urges Christians to confess their transgressions before gathering on the Lord's Day so that their eucharistic sacrifice may be pure (ch. 14). What the *Didache* envisions is probably an individual confession of sins to God before coming to church, as part of one's personal preparation to gather with others in church. James here envisions a similar confession of sins on the part of the sick, but in the presence of the presbyters who visit him to pray and anoint him.

It may be thought that the elders of the church may not be able to effect such a cure. But James assures his hearers that **the working** or effectual **supplication of a righteous man has much strength**. The elders may be no more holy than the others (especially if some unrighteous ones have been ordained; see 3:14). But one does not require the supernatural sanctity of the angels to pray effectively. God is able to hear the prayers of mortals as well.

Elijah, for example, **was a man of like-nature to us, and he prayed with prayer** (i.e. prayed fervently) **that it might not rain**. Only God can give or withhold the rain (Deut. 28:12, 23). Yet even so, when the man Elijah prayed for drought as God's judgment on Israel, there was drought, and **it did not rain upon the earth for three years and six months** (3 Kg. 17; 18 LXX)—an amazingly long time, and proof of divine power. It was only after **he prayed again** that **the heaven gave rain, and the earth sprouted its fruit**. Clearly, men on earth can effectually avail with the God of heaven, and one should not disdain the united prayers of the presbyters.

In all situations of life, therefore, whether in hardship, in good times, or in sickness, one should turn to God, referring all things to Him.

§IX.   Exhortation to Reclaim the Sinner (5:19–20)

ৡ৵ ৡ৵ ৡ৵ ৡ৵ ৡ৵

19 My brothers, if anyone among you strays from the truth, and anyone turns him back,

20 let him know that he who turns a sinner from the deception of his way will save his soul from death, and will cover a multitude of sins.

James concludes his epistle with an exhortation to reclaim the sinner. If persecution, hardship, or sickness have driven **anyone** of them from God, so that one **strays from the truth** of the Gospel, they should do all things possible to win him back. The community should not simply turn a blind eye to the defection and loss of one of their own. Like the Savior who calls all impious sinners to Himself, one should strive to persuade the apostate brother to return.

Let the reclaiming brother be assured of his reward. If he succeeds, through private prayer to God and earnest appeal to the apostate, he will not only **save** the sinner's **soul from death**, but will also **cover a multitude of** his own **sins**.

James's statement about covering (or winning forgiveness for) a multitude of one's own sins should be interpreted against the Jewish background of such passages as Sirach 3:30, "Almsgiving atones for sin," and Tobit 12:9, "Almsgiving . . . will purge away every sin." That is, pious almsgiving brings God's blessing, so that (for example) when sickness strikes, God will not judge the pious sick man for his sins, but will forgive and heal him. James here asserts that reclaiming the wandering brother is a truly pious act and one that wins such forgiveness from God. Reclaiming one's erring brother is a good work, and the one doing it will be blessed in his doing (1:25). As Origen said in his commentary on Leviticus, "A man who converts others will have his own sins forgiven."

The epistle of James ends on this note of hope. In one's walk of faith, there are many trials: persecution, hardship, sickness. Many temptations rise up to divert us from our way: temptations not to actualize our faith by good works, to indulge in sinful partiality to the rich, to misuse our tongue to quarrel and condemn. But should we veer from the true path, the way of repentance and salvation always remains open. James encourages the faithful to help one another home along this way, thereby not only saving the erring brother, but winning God's grace for ourselves as well.

✖ The First Epistle of St. Peter ✖

Introduction

St. Peter, like the rest of the Twelve of whom he was the leader, vanishes from the view of recorded history because he obeyed his Lord. The Lord directed him to go and make disciples of all nations (Matt. 28:19), and so he went, leaving his whereabouts a mystery to future generations of historians.

Peter is prominent in the first half of Luke's Acts of the Apostles. He preaches in Jerusalem and Palestine and brings the Gospel to the Gentiles of Caesarea. He is arrested by Herod's men and miraculously released. And then he is gone. After Peter's miraculous escape from prison and his visit to the brethren to tell them of this, Luke next records, "Then he departed and went to another place" (Acts 12:17). That's all we hear about Peter until we catch up with him in Rome, writing two epistles and finally being martyred under Nero in about AD 65. For Peter, obeying his Lord and bringing the Gospel to all the world was more important than leaving a detailed account of how he did it.

The mystery surrounding Peter's itinerary surrounds his epistles as well. When did he write them? Did he ever visit the communities to which he writes? Did he write the epistles himself or use an amanuensis?

In the absence of sure evidence, I would offer the following.

It seems that Peter wrote his first epistle by the hand of Silvanus (called Silas in Acts 15:40). While it is possible that a Galilean fisherman wrote such good Greek (using the Greek Septuagint for his Old Testament citations), it is more likely that the polished Greek is the result of using a secretary. If Silvanus was indeed the actual writer, this would also account for the Pauline feel of much of the letter, for Silvanus was the friend of St. Paul. The phrase in 1 Peter

57

5:12 *can* mean "delivered by Silvanus," but it can also mean "written by Silvanus" (Eusebius uses the same phrase in his *History of the Church*, 4.23, to indicate the Roman church "writing through Clement"—i.e. with Clement as the actual writer).

I would suggest that Peter dictated the letter (possibly in Aramaic), giving Silvanus abundant editorial freedom to phrase it as he wished in Greek. If this is so, it would also account for the difference in Greek styles between the first epistle of Peter and the second epistle, for the Greek of the first epistle is much better. It is possible that Silvanus was also the bearer of the epistle.

The place of writing is certain: the letter was written from Rome (called "Babylon" in 5:13).

The epistle was sent as a circular to Christians in the backwoods of the empire: in Pontus, Galatia, Cappadocia, Asia, and Bithynia. It is possible that Peter visited such communities on his way to Rome and wrote to them on the strength of these previous contacts. It is equally possible that Peter had not been there, but their situation was made known to him by Silvanus (who had accompanied Paul to Galatia; Acts 16:6), and that it was Silvanus who urged Peter to write to them. It is also possible that, since all roads led to Rome, another anonymous Christian from those places came to Rome with news of the Christians there, and that Peter wrote at the request of this anonymous brother.

The date of the epistle may be fixed fairly precisely. Paul was imprisoned in Rome about 60, and released two years later in 62. Peter is not mentioned by Luke in his Acts as being in Rome during this time, nor does Paul mention Peter in his letters written during his imprisonment, so it seems as if Peter did not arrive in Rome until after Paul had left. The Great Fire of Rome occurred in July 64, with Peter executed in the persecution that followed it. That would place Peter's arrival in Rome after 62 and before 64. I would suggest Peter arrived in Rome in about the summer of 63, and that he wrote this first epistle around the winter of 63 or the spring of 64.

Opposition to the Christians at that time was growing throughout the empire (so that Nero found them a convenient scapegoat), but that opposition had not yet produced an official state-led persecution at the time of writing. That would come only after the Great Fire of Rome. Peter wrote this epistle to Christians who were being pressured because of their faith, and who needed encouragement to persevere and instruction on how to interact with an increasingly hostile society.

In our day, when Christians are increasingly under pressure from secular forces, Peter's words have a timely ring to them. We also need to hear these words from Peter, chief of the apostles and martyr for the Lord.

❧ The First Epistle of St. Peter ❧

§I.   Opening Greeting (1:1–2)

❧ ❧ ❧ ❧ ❧

1 1   Peter, an apostle of Jesus Christ, to the chosen exiles of the Diaspora of Pontus, Galatia,
Cappadocia, Asia, and Bithynia,

2   *chosen* according to the foreknowledge of God
the Father, in the sanctification of the Spirit,
for obedience and sprinkling with the blood of
Jesus Christ: may grace and peace be multiplied
to you.

Peter, although writing to Gentiles, in this epistle applies to
them the titles which had characterized the Jews, since these Gen-
tiles, through their faith, had become part of God's People. The
Jews living outside Palestine were called **the Diaspora** (compare
John 7:35), and Peter refers to the recipients of his letter living in
Pontus, Galatia, Cappadocia, Asia, and Bithynia by this classic
Jewish title. Like the Jews of old, these Gentiles were now God's
chosen people. But, unlike the Jews, their true homeland was not
Palestine, but heaven, and while living on earth, they were **exiles**
from their true home.

The order of the places Peter lists is significant, for it represents
the order in which the bearer of the letter would reach them as he
traveled down the Roman roads from Rome.

In addressing these Gentiles, Peter does not simply offer greetings. Rather, he reminds them of how God has changed them and
of their true dignity. Though they are under pressure to conform

to the world around them, they must remember who they now are and refuse to conform.

For they are part of this world no longer, for **God the Father**, the Maker of all men, has *chosen* them **according to** His **fore-knowledge**. That is, God knew from the foundation of the world who would be humble and open-hearted, and these He transforms in holy baptism, making them His sons through Christ.

This baptismal conversion occurs **in the sanctification of the Spirit**. The term *sanctification* here refers to the change from dark-ness to light, to the convert's passage from the power of Satan to God. They are sanctified in that they now belong to God (see 1 Cor. 6:11), and this transformation of regeneration is accomplished by **the Spirit**.

The result of this baptismal regeneration is their **obedience and sprinkling with the blood of Jesus Christ**. Formerly, as pagans, they disobeyed God and did not keep His Law, but now they live in **obedience** and strive after righteousness. And just as the people of Israel were sprinkled with the blood of sacrifice after they entered into covenant with God (Ex. 24:5–8), so these Gentile Christians were **sprinkled with the blood of Jesus Christ** and cleansed of their sins. This **sprinkling** refers to the shed blood of Jesus, which cleanses His disciples as they partake of His sacrifice in the Holy Eucharist (see Heb. 9:13–14; 10:19–25; 12:24).

Their baptism leads them to a life of continued obedience and cleansing, thus making them different from the world around them. It is to these saints that Peter desires God to **multiply** His **grace and peace**.

§II.   Our Hope as God's Redeemed (1:3—2:10)

The Greatness of Our Hope

> ֍ ֍ ֍ ֍ ֍
>
> 3   Blessed *be* the God and Father of our Lord Jesus
>   Christ, who according to His great mercy has
>   regenerated us to a living hope through the
>   resurrection of Jesus Christ from the dead,

4   to *receive* an inheritance incorruptible and unde-
     filed and unfading, kept in the heavens for you,

5   who are guarded by the power of God through
     faith for a salvation prepared to be revealed in
     the last *appointed* time,

6   in which *hope* you exult, even though now for
     a little *while*, if necessary, you have been made
     sorrowful by various testings,

7   that the proof of your faith, more precious
     than perishing gold, even though *the gold is*
     proven by fire, may be found *to result* in praise
     and glory and honor at the revelation of Jesus
     Christ,

8   whom not having seen, you love, and though
     you do not see Him now, but believe in Him,
     you exult with inexpressible and glorified joy,

9   receiving back as the end of your faith the salva-
     tion of souls,

10   about which salvation, the prophets who
     prophesied of the grace *that would come* to
     you sought out and examined out,

11   examining *to discover* who or what kind of
     appointed time the Spirit of Christ within them
     was *making* plain as He pre-witnessed to the
     sufferings of Christ and the glories after these
     things,

12   to whom was revealed that they were not serv-
     ing themselves but you, in these things which
     now have been announced to you through those
     who preached *the good news* to you by the Holy
     Spirit sent from heaven—things into which the
     angels desire to peer.

Peter addresses converts who feel the pressure of the world upon
them, and so he begins by reminding them of the great reward
awaiting them if they resist this pressure and cling to their faith in

Christ. Letters in those days customarily began with a prayer or thanksgiving, and Peter begins with such a prayer. But the greatness of God's mercy carries him away, and the sentence begun in verse 3 does not come to an end until the end of verse 12.

In his opening prayer, Peter explodes in thanksgiving, declaring, **Blessed** *be* **God**, for God is the One who manifested His love for men in the Gospel as the **Father of our Lord Jesus Christ**. For **according to His great mercy** upon those who had no claim on His favor, He **regenerated us**, granting new birth in baptism (compare Titus 3:5, where baptism is called "the washing of regeneration"). This regeneration came to the new converts **through the resurrection of Jesus Christ from the dead**. That is, the risen life of Christ was bestowed on them in baptism, so that they now share the power of that resurrection (compare Rom. 6:4–5). This baptism also bestowed on them **a living hope**, the certainty that they will *receive* **an inheritance** of life and joy in the age to come. This hope is called **living** because it is certain and braces the heart.

Here is an inheritance to look forward to! It is **incorruptible**, **undefiled**, **unfading**. (Peter uses three negative words, for the glory of the inheritance strains the limits of conceptual language.) The inheritance is described as **incorruptible** (Gr. *aphthartos*), for the glory given to us will be immortal, as God is immortal (Rom. 1:23). It is **undefiled** (Gr. *amiantos*), for it remains pristine, unsullied, awaiting the time when we will inherit it. It is **unfading** (Gr. *amarantos*), for the passage of countless ages will not dim its brilliance. This inheritance and reward is **kept** by God **in the heavens** for them, out of the reach of persecuting men. They may rest assured that their inheritance is safe and will be there for them when they reach the end. And they may be confident of safely reaching the end. In moments of persecution, they may be tempted to think of themselves as vulnerable and weak, and to think that God has abandoned them. This is not so. Rather, they are **guarded by the power of God** Himself, so that they will inherit the **salvation** that has already been **prepared** for them and is even now ready **to be revealed in the last** *appointed* **time**, at the Second Coming. His power guards them **through faith**, and as long as they cling to their confession of Jesus, God will bring them to a triumphant end in His Kingdom. Let them be bold and confess Christ before all the world, for if they do, God will see them safely home. The persecutors might take their property and even their lives, but they cannot really touch them (compare Luke 21:16–18).

Thus, they can **exult** and leap for joy, **even though now, if necessary** (that is, if God's providence thinks it best), they must be **made sorrowful by various testings**, such as slander, ostracism, and other forms of persecution. Though hard to endure, the persecution of this age is really only **for a little** *while* compared to the ages of glory that follow, and so may be easily borne. The sufferings of persecution are thus like the flames of a crucible (see Wisdom 3:5–6). Just as **perishing gold** is **proven by fire**, so **the proof of** their **faith**, which is even **more precious** than gold, is in their sufferings. Gold must pass through the fire to be proven and found pure of alloy, and so their faith also must pass through the flames if it is to **be found** to result in **praise and glory and honor** for them **at the revelation of Jesus Christ** on the Last Day.

And that final **revelation of Jesus Christ** will be wonderful. **Not having seen** Him in their life and **not seeing Him** even **now**, they still **love** Him and **believe in Him**, and **exult with inexpressible and glorified joy**. That is, even though they do not now see Him, they rejoice with a joy that defies description, a joy that partakes of the glory of heaven. How much more then will they exult and rejoice when they finally see Him face to face? Because of this **faith** and love for Jesus, they will **receive back** as their faith's **end** and goal **the salvation of** their **souls**. By *soul* (Gr. *psuche*), Peter means their life (compare the use of the term in Mark 8:35; Luke 12:22); the world may insist that Christians are wasting their lives in the service of Jesus, but Peter asserts that they are saving them.

This salvation is so great that even **the prophets who prophesied** in the Old Testament Scriptures **sought out and examined out** the whole issue, searching their own utterances *to discover* **who or what kind of** *appointed* **time the Spirit within them was** *making* plain. The Spirit is here called the **Spirit of Christ**, because the Spirit, speaking through the prophets, **pre-witnessed to the sufferings of Christ and the glories** of His exaltation that would follow **after these** sufferings. He is called the Spirit of Christ because He predicted the things that occurred through Jesus of Nazareth.

The words rendered *sought out* and *examined out* are intensive; *seek out* is the Greek *ekzeteo*, an intensive form of *zeteo*, "to seek"; *examine out* is the Greek *exeraunao*, an intensive form of *eraunao*, "to examine, to search, to investigate." These intensives show how greatly the prophets wanted to discover whether this **grace** and salvation was to come to them in their day. The salvation was so wonderful, they could hardly wait! But it **was revealed** to them by God **that they were not serving themselves** and their own generation. Rather, they were serving Peter's hearers, those living in the Christian era, who are recipients of what has **now been announced through those who preached** *the good news*. The wonderful salvation the prophets predicted has come to pass in the lives of Peter's hearers.

Peter refers to the good news of Jesus as preached **by** the power of **the Holy Spirit sent from heaven**. The reference is to the Day of Pentecost, when the Spirit was first sent by Christ upon His Church (Acts 2:1f; John 16:7), the Spirit who ever abides in the Church and is received through Holy Baptism and Chrismation. Peter stresses that the Gospel is preached by the apostles by the Spirit's power to show that the new age predicted by the prophets has begun. The same Spirit who gave the prophecies in ancient times now inspires the apostles to interpret them correctly as being fulfilled in Jesus.

Peter ends his description of the greatness of their salvation (and his long sentence) by saying that it is into such glorious things that **the angels desire to peer**. The word translated *peer* is the Greek *parakupto*, translated as "stoop" in John 20:5. The salvation of the Christians is so wonderful that even the angels watching from heaven long to bend down for a better look and see all the details of their salvation's fulfillment. What a great privilege therefore is theirs!

The Call to Live as God's Redeemed

ക്ക ക്ക ക്ക ക്ക ക്ക

13 Therefore, gird up the loins of your minds, be sober, hope perfectly on the grace being brought to you at the revelation of Jesus Christ.

14 As obedient children, do not be conformed to the former desires *which were yours* in your ignorance,

15 but like the Holy One who called you, become holy yourselves also in all your conduct,

16 because it is written, "You shall be holy for I *Myself am* holy."

17 And if you call upon *as* Father the One who impartially judges according to each one's work, conduct *yourselves* in fear during the time of your sojourn,

18 knowing that you were not redeemed with corruptible *things* like silver or gold from your useless conduct delivered from your forefathers,

19 but with precious blood, as of a blameless and spotless lamb, *the blood* of Christ,

20 who was foreknown before the foundation of the world, but was manifested in the last times for the sake of you

21 who through Him are believers in God, the One who raised Him from the dead and gave Him glory, that your faith and hope might be in God.

Having reminded his hearers of the greatness of the salvation waiting for them, he **therefore** urges them to live consistently with their status as the redeemed of God. The *therefore* of verse 13 refers back to the thought of verses 3–12.

They are urged to **gird up the loins of** their **minds**. The image of "girding up" presupposes the clothing of that day. People wore long, loose, flowing robes, and before they could do any work, they would gather the robe and tuck it into their belt so that they would not trip. In urging his hearers to **gird up the loins of** their **minds**, Peter urges them to prepare their minds for action. The world will challenge them, and they must prepare themselves to meet the challenge by being **sober**, and by **hoping perfectly on the grace being brought to** them **at the revelation of Jesus Christ**.

The word rendered *be sober* is the Greek *nepho*, which refers not just to physical sobriety (that is, the absence of drunkenness), but also to self-control, maintaining an inner vigilance and balance. The world can provoke a sense of excitement, of agitation, even of panic, and the Christian must keep his head.

As well as this inner composure, the Christian meets the world's challenge by **hoping perfectly on the grace being brought** him by Christ at His Second Coming. That is, the Christian fixes his hope completely on the favor and glory that Christ will bestow upon him when He comes. Thus, when the world tempts him to sin, he is strengthened to resist as he thinks of the reward his enduring righteousness will win.

In baptism they were called to be God's **obedient children** as they became His sons. They must live out their baptism and **not be conformed to the former desires**, which were theirs in their **ignorance** as pagans when they did not know the living God. The **desires** of lust, greed, malice must be indulged no longer. The world would like to squeeze them into its mold, forcing them to live as they used to live before they knew God and His demands. This they must not consent to. Instead, **like the Holy One** of Israel **who called** them in their baptism, they must **become holy** themselves **in all** their daily **conduct**. That is why **it is written, "You shall be holy for I** *Myself* *am* **holy"** (see Lev. 11:44). When God called them in baptism to become His children, He called them to share His holiness, so that as children they resemble their Father.

They can understand the necessity for this themselves when they remember their weekly post-baptismal worship. In that worship they invoke and **call upon** God *as* **Father** (such as when they say the "Our Father"), yet He is **the One who impartially judges according to each one's work**. If they invite into their midst such an impartial Judge, they must **conduct** themselves **in fear during the time of** their **sojourn** in this age, for He will show no favoritism to them. If they sin grievously, He will judge and condemn them, both in this age (compare 1 Cor. 11:29–31) and at the Last Judgment. Let them therefore fear to sin, and be holy in their daily conduct.

There is, however, a more compelling reason to avoid sin than fear of judgment. That is, they are **not redeemed with corruptible** *things* **like silver or gold from** the **useless conduct delivered from** their **forefathers**. They were once enslaved to idols and bound by fear of death, walking every day in the **useless** and empty **conduct** or way of life which was **delivered** to them by tradition from their pagan ancestors. All of their idolatrous rituals led only to death. The true God has **redeemed** them and bought them back from this slavery. But the price of this ransom is not **silver** or even **gold**, the usual way slaves were bought back. Rather, they were ransomed **with precious blood, as of a blameless and spotless lamb**, namely, the blood **of Christ**. Christ shed His blood to buy them back for God and bring them to life. Gratitude for this sacrifice is an even more potent incentive to righteousness than fear of judgment. Christ, the **blameless and spotless Lamb**, offered His life for them—how can they live in such a way as to nullify that holy sacrifice?

The world may think that Jesus and His movement are just another part of the rise and fall of history, and that the Christian movement will fade like other merely historical movements of the time. But it is otherwise, for Jesus **was foreknown before the foundation of the world**. That is, God knew before the world began what He would do through His Christ. Jesus' work was part of the plan God had from the beginning and has **manifested** now **in the last times**. The Christian movement is not to fade like other movements resembling it.

It is through this movement that Peter's Gentile hearers are **believers in God** (that is, in the God **who raised** Jesus **from the dead and gave Him glory**). Before Jesus appeared, the Gentiles remained separated from the Jews, lost in useless pagan ways of life. Now even the Gentiles are brought to the true God. The old ways of the world are breaking down, as God through Christ has created a new humanity (Eph. 2:13–16). Through Jesus, their **faith and hope** are now **in** the true **God**.

ॐ ॐ ॐ ॐ ॐ

22 Having in obedience to the truth purified your souls for an unhypocritical brotherly-love, fervently love one another from the heart,

23 for you have been regenerated not from corruptible seed, but incorruptible *seed*, through the living and remaining Word of God.

24 Because "all flesh *is* as grass, and all its glory as the flower of grass. The grass was dried up, and the flower falls off,

25 "but the Word of the Lord remains to the ages." And this is the Word which was preached *as good news* to you.

Since they have been so redeemed, and have in **obedience to the truth** of the Gospel **purified** their **souls** in baptism **for an unhypocritical brotherly-love**, let them fulfill this baptismal obedience and **fervently love one another from the heart**. Community is the purpose of their incorporation into Christ. They have **purified** their whole lives (or **souls**, Gr. *psuche*) for the purpose of mutual love in the Lord. Peter here thinks primarily of love between Christians in community (Gr. *philadephia*), rather than love for outsiders (though of course this is good too). His main focus is love for the brotherhood (compare 2:17) and the preservation of Christian unity.

This love and unity are important because their baptism made them all brothers, united by indestructible bonds of brotherhood. For they **have been regenerated** in baptism, **not from corruptible seed, but incorruptible *seed*, through the living and remaining Word of God**. Men received natural birth from **seed** which is **corruptible** and mortal, and merely natural life on earth will eventually end. The **seed** which gives new birth is **incorruptible**, and it begins a life that will never end, for the seed is the **Word** of the Gospel; it is **living** and eternal; it **remains** and abides forever. The ties of kinship that unite the Christians therefore surpass anything on earth.

This is what Isaiah 40:6–8 means when it says, **"all flesh *is* as grass, and all its glory as the flower of grass. The grass was dried up, and the flower falls off, but the Word of the Lord remains to the ages."** **All flesh**, all life in this age, with all its flowery pagan pomp, is as transient as the **grass** of the field. For all its apparent beauty and **glory**, soon it is **dried up**, and its glory **falls off**. Beauty fades, strength fails, all men die. **But the Word of the Lord remains to the ages**, and the life it gives never dies. Peter adds that this **Word of the Lord**, spoken of by Isaiah, is the very **Word** of the Gospel **which was preached *as good news*** to them. They must love one another, for that Gospel bestowed a birth and a common kinship that is eternal and makes them different from the world.

ৡ৵ ৡ৵ ৡ৵ ৡ৵ ৡ৵

2 1 Therefore, putting off all wickedness and all guile and hypocrisies and envies and all evil-speakings,

2 as newborn infants, long for the guileless rational milk, that by it you may grow for salvation,

3 if you have tasted that the Lord *is* kind.

4 And coming to Him *as to* a living stone, rejected by men but chosen and honored in *the sight* of God,

5 you also, as living stones, are being built up as a spiritual house for a holy priesthood, to offer spiritual sacrifices well-accepted by God through Jesus Christ.

6 For it is contained in Scripture: "Behold, I lay in Zion a chosen honored cornerstone, and he who believes on Him will not be put to shame."

> 7 The honor, therefore, *is* for you who believe.
> But for those who disbelieve, "The stone which
> the builders rejected, this has become the head
> of the corner," and "a stumbling stone and a
> rock of offense"; for they stumble because they
> are disobedient to the Word, to which they were
> also set.
>
> 9 But you *yourselves are* a chosen race, a royal
> priesthood, a holy nation, a people for *His* own
> acquisition, that you may declare-out the vir-
> tues of Him who has called you from darkness
> into His marvelous light,
>
> 10 who once *were* not a people, but now *are the*
> people of God; *you* had not received mercy, but
> now have received mercy.

Because they have been regenerated in baptism for the purpose of forming a loving community, they **therefore** must **put off** all that remains of the old ways that would harm that community. Even as they put off their clothes in preparation for baptism, they must now put aside sins against love.

In particular, they must have done with **all wickedness** and malice (Gr. *kakia*), the ill will that poisons fellowship. They must renounce **all guile** (Gr. *dolos*), all manipulation, all words springing from ulterior motives. Also, they must shun **hypocrisies** (Gr. *upokriseis*, in the plural), acts of insincerity whereby we feign a loving attitude but act spitefully behind someone's back. They must have done with **envies** (Gr. *phthonous*, in the plural), acts of jealous rivalry in which we try to come off better than our neighbor. Last on the list of vices to be renounced is **all evil-speakings** (Gr. *kata-lalias*, also in the plural), which include acts of slander, criticism, and misrepresentation. It is fatally easy to cloak such sins in high-sounding names and to let them survive in our Christian life. But such things destroy the brotherly-love which is the goal of baptism.

Having renounced such sins, **as newborn infants** fresh from the baptismal womb and new to the life in Christ, they should

long for the **milk** which Mother Church provides. Just as babies insistently cry for milk as the only way they can grow and thrive, so should Peter's hearers just as insistently seek the true milk, as the only way they **may grow for salvation** and reach the Kingdom—**if** (Peter adds, alluding to Ps. 34:8) they **have tasted that the Lord** *is* **kind** and how good that milk is. Assuming that they have truly experienced for themselves how sweet the ways of holiness are, Peter says, doubtless they will want more!

The milk that enables them to grow is described as **guileless** and **rational.** The word rendered *guileless* is the Greek *adolos*, which comes from *dolos*, "guile," the word used in verse 1. It describes milk that is pure, undiluted, not deceptively watered down, as some milk was. The thought is of Christian teaching that is pure, free of secular philosophy, for such syncretistic teaching would deceive the heart.

The milk (or teaching) is also described as **rational**, in the Greek *logikos*. This Greek word is cognate with *logos*, which is rendered "word, reason, rationality." It here describes milk that is nonmaterial, spiritual, that given by the Word (*Logos*) of God. This is what the believers are to seek after—teaching that is pure, spiritual, coming from the apostolic tradition and free of all worldly mixture.

This teaching is available at the assemblies of the Church, and they must come to Christ there. He is the **living stone, rejected by men but chosen and honored in** *the sight* **of God**. Peter here alludes to Psalm 118:22 and Isaiah 28:16. Christ in Mark 12:10 applies to Himself the image of the **stone, rejected by men** of the world as worthless and a stone no good for building, but which God **chose** to be the **honored** cornerstone on which the whole building depends. For the world rejects Christ as a deluded deceiver and cannot understand how a crucified carpenter can be the power of God. In the same way, the world rejects the Christians as deluded and cannot understand how they can live and die for this Man.

But as Christ is the **living stone** (for He is the source of eternal life), so the believers are **living stones** (for they have received that life from Him), and they are to **come to Him** week by week for the

Eucharist to receive teaching and new life. As they do that, they are **being built up** by God **as a spiritual house**, a temple **for a holy priesthood**, the dwelling place of God Himself. The weekly gathering of the Christians is not (as the pagans think) a place where the misfits assemble. Rather, it is the place where God manifests Himself, dwelling in the Christians by His Spirit.

Reference to the holy priesthood leads Peter to combine this metaphor with his previous one. The Christians gathered are not only God's temple, they are the **holy priesthood** that ministers in the temple. In their weekly Eucharists, they **offer spiritual sacrifices well-accepted by God through Jesus Christ**. The sacrifices of other men are the bodies and blood of animals, but the sacrifices of the Christians are **spiritual** (Gr. *pneumatikos*), consisting of praise, the doxological thanksgiving and memorial of the Cross and Resurrection of Christ.

Peter's reference to Jesus as **the living stone** is confirmed by citing **Scripture: "Behold, I lay in Zion a chosen honored cornerstone, and he who believes on Him will not be put to shame"** (Is. 28:16). Jesus is the **honored** stone that brings salvation, the **cornerstone** of the new Temple, and **he who believes on Him will not be put to shame** on the Last Day. But **the honor** and the inclusion in the new Temple are only for those **who believe**. Those who encounter Him with proud hearts and **who disbelieve** will not find salvation. The new spiritual Temple is not for them to worship in.

Jesus is indeed the Stone of God, but for these proud ones, He will be **"the stone which the builders rejected"** (Ps. 118:22), Him whom they despise and refuse. For them He will prove **"a stumbling stone and a rock of offense"** (Is. 8:14). They will stumble and fall over this stone and be cast eternally headlong. Their condemnation results not from any fault in Jesus the Stone, but because they **are disobedient to the Word** of the Gospel, and to this fate **they were also set** by God. It is not, however, that God overrides their free will, so that they have no choice but to disobey and reject the Gospel. Rather, it is that in His providence, God decreed that the proud should find their judgment and doom by stumbling over One who came in humility. Their proud hearts are ready to stumble (compare Prov. 16:18), and Christ provides the occasion for their fall. Peter stresses this to show that it all depends on whether one believes or disbelieves (v. 7). The believer's faith is central to his salvation (compare 1:5, 9)—let his hearers cling to their faith!

For they are not destined for doom. Unlike the unbelievers, they (the pronoun is emphatic in the Greek) are **a chosen race, a royal priesthood, a holy nation, a people for** God's **own acquisition**. He called them in baptism and made them His own so that they might **declare-out** in their worship and in their daily life **the virtues** and glory **of Him who has called** them **from** the **darkness** of paganism and death **into His marvelous** and miraculous **light**. The word rendered *marvelous* is the Greek *thaumastos*, cognate with *thauma*, "wonder, miracle." The light and life of His Kingdom into which God called them are remarkable indeed. The change is truly astonishing!

In describing these Gentiles as **a chosen race, a royal priesthood, a holy nation, a people for** God's **own acquisition** who will **declare-out** His **virtues**, Peter applies the titles given to Israel in the Greek version of Isaiah 43:20–21; Exodus 19:5–6; 23:22, for the Church is the true Israel. They are now God's **chosen race** of people, different from all the peoples of the world. They are His **royal priesthood**, set apart as a community with access to His presence. They are **a holy nation**, protected by God, who watches over His holy ones (compare Ps. 105:14–15). They are **a people for** *His* **own acquisition**, His very own treasure, valued and guarded by Him.

Thus these Gentiles are separated from God no longer. While they were pagans, they were **not a people** with any dignity, but **now** they are the **people of God**. Once they **had not received mercy**, but were destined for the wrath reserved for idolaters; but **now** they **have received mercy** as God's chosen people. (Once again Peter cites Hos. 1:10; 2:23, applying these titles of Israel to the Gentile converts.) In Christ God has united them to Himself and made them His own people. They belong to the pagan world no longer.

§III.   Living among the Gentiles (2:11—4:11)

Exhortation to Live as Sojourners among the Gentiles

ॐ ॐ ॐ ॐ ॐ

11 Beloved, I exhort *you* as sojourners and exiles
to abstain from fleshly desires, which soldier
against the soul.

12 Have good conduct among the Gentiles, so that
wherein they speak against you as evildoers,
they may by your good works, as they observe
them, glorify God in the day of visitation.

St. Peter now begins a new section, addressing his hearers as
beloved because of his pastoral care for them in the Lord. It is important that these Gentiles think of themselves as different from the
secular world around them and as belonging now to the Kingdom
of God. Therefore Peter **exhorts** them **as sojourners and exiles** on
earth to live differently from their pagan neighbors. Sojourners are
those who live in one place although they were born and belong
elsewhere, and who therefore do not fit in with their present sur-
roundings. They can always be recognized by the natives as foreigners.
Peter urges his hearers to recognize that since their baptism they now
no longer fit in with the pagan culture surrounding them.

This culture is characterized by **fleshly desires** and sinful practices such as lust, greed, gluttony, and drunkenness. As those who
now belong to the Kingdom, they must **abstain** from these, since
these desires **soldier** and wage war **against the soul**. Indulging
such appetites may seem to lead to fulfillment and happiness, but
it actually leads to death. True life consists in righteousness and
in avoiding such practices. The term *soul* (Gr. *psuche*) here refers
to the entire living person, not to the immaterial spirit as opposed
to the body. The thought is that indulging such desires wars against
the person's own good and true life.

Abstaining from fleshly desires and **having good conduct
among the Gentiles** also accomplishes something else. (We note in

passing that Peter writes to his audience as if they were not Gentiles themselves, for through Christ they have left this age and are a new creation.) In a number of instances their Gentile neighbors **speak against** them **as evildoers**. The Christians indeed tend to withdraw from the drunken parties and other social activities characteristic of Gentile life (compare 4:4), and they have gained a reputation as antisocial haters of mankind as a result. They are further accused of such atrocities as incest, murder, and cannibalism (from a garbled understanding of Christian talk of "eating the Body and drinking the Blood" and of "the Kiss" [i.e. the Kiss of Peace] exchanged among "the brothers and sisters").

Peter says that by doing **good works** they can help reverse that judgment, so that as their neighbors **observe** their works they may perhaps come to repent and become believers themselves, and so **glorify God in the day of visitation** and judgment on the Last Day. Works such as almsgiving, feeding and clothing the poor, and taking in society's castoffs thus have an evangelistic value as well.

Submission in Relationships

ॐ ॐ ॐ ॐ ॐ

13 Submit for the Lord's sake to every human creation, whether to a king as the one surpassing *all*,

14 or to governors as sent by him for avenging on evildoers and praise of good-doers.

15 For thus is the will of God, that by doing-good you may muzzle the ignorance of senseless men,

16 *living* as free men, and not having the freedom as a covering of wickedness, but as slaves of God.

17 Honor all; love the brotherhood; fear God; honor the king.

In their interaction with the society around them, Peter then urges them to **submit for the Lord's sake to every human**

creation. The word rendered *creation* is the Greek *ktisis*, elsewhere used for the creation of the world and all those in it (Rom. 1:20; 8:39). He uses this word to show that even in pagan society, those who demand our submission are still the **creation** of God, and so if we submit to them **for the Lord's sake**, it is a way of submitting to Him. The Christians are tempted to refuse this submission because those demanding it are pagan. (This is all the more so in the case of the emperor, whose cult demands not only submission, but worship.) Peter writes to tell his readers that proper submission to the authorities is lawful for Christians.

That applies not only to the **king** (or emperor) **as the one surpassing** *all* in authority, but also **to governors**, since they are **sent by him**. This submission to governing authorities should present no moral dilemma, since the local authorities' task is preservation of public order, consisting in **avenging on evildoers and praise of good-doers**. The two terms *evildoer* (Gr. *kakopoieo*) and *good-doer* (*agathopoieo*) refer respectively to those who commit crimes and those who help the community. The avenging and punishment of criminals and rewarding of public benefactors is the task of government, and Christians should submit to it to help fulfill these worthy goals.

In this way they will also fulfill **the will of God**. That is, **by doing-good** (Gr. *agathopoieo*) they will **muzzle** and silence **the ignorance of senseless men**. Their foes accuse them of all sorts of crimes, but the Christians' good works will demonstrate that their charges are ignorant and uninformed, and thus will shut them up.

Some Christians may feel their spiritual freedom is demeaned by submission to such pagan rulers. (The Jewish Zealots felt this very keenly.) But Peter insists this is not so. They are indeed living **as free men**, but must not **have** that **freedom as a covering of wickedness**. Those who protest that it is demeaning to submit to legal authorities usually are not motivated by noble aims, and their desire for **freedom** is simply a pretext and **covering** for doing **wickedness**. Christians, though free men, have their spiritual freedom rooted in being the **slaves of God**, and slaves should not find obedience demeaning. They must not let their spiritual freedom be reduced to moral licentiousness.

Thus, as slaves they should settle it in their minds to **honor all**, giving to each one the appropriate respect. (The verb *honor* is in the aorist, probably indicating this once-for-all determination.)

This basic principle works itself out in various ways. (The following verbs are all in the present tense, denoting continuing attitudes.) They must **love the brotherhood**, their fellow Christians. The Christians are called **the brotherhood** (Gr. *adelphotes*) because all believers are spiritual kin, with the obligations of loyalty that obtain in families. They must **fear God**, giving to Him first of all the worship due Him. There is here possibly an oblique reference to the cult of emperor worship, with Peter warning his hearers not to give to the emperor the honor due to God alone. Last of all, they must **honor the king**, giving to the emperor his proper respect. It is probably significant that the king comes last in this list, after obligations to love their fellow believers and to fear God. The king has his proper place, but it comes after these other and eternal priorities.

☙ ☙ ☙ ☙ ☙

18 House-*slaves*, submit to your masters in all fear, not only to the good and forbearing ones, but also to the crooked ones.

19 For this finds grace, if for the sake of conscience toward God a man endures under sorrows when suffering unjustly.

20 For what fame *is there* if, when you sin and are buffeted, you persevere? But if when you do good and suffer you persevere, this *finds* grace with God.

21 For to this *purpose* you have been called, because Christ also suffered for you, leaving behind a model for you, that you may follow after in His steps,

22 who did no sin, nor was guile found in His mouth,

23 who while being abused, did not counter-abuse; while suffering, did not threaten, but delivered

---

> Himself over to the One judging righteously;
> 24 who Himself carried our sins in His body upon
> the tree, that we, having departed from the sins,
> might live to righteousness, by whose welts you
> were cured.
> 25 For you were straying as sheep, but now you
> have returned to the Shepherd and Bishop of
> your souls.

House-*slaves* (Gr. *oiketes*) are singled out for special attention, not only because of their great numbers, but also because of their special temptations to despise authority. They are told to **submit to** their **masters**, which they must do **in all fear** of God, submitting to their masters for God's sake. (Peter in this epistle always uses the word *fear*, Gr. *phobos*, for the fear of God, telling Christians not to fear men; compare 3:14.) Such an exhortation is needed because of the slave's temptation to submit if the master is **good and forbearing**, but to disobey when the master is **crooked** and unreasonable in his demands (Gr. *skolios*, "bent, perverse"). Such harsh treatment is perhaps especially a possibility for Christian slaves as Christians become more and more socially despised.

If the house-slave **for the sake of conscience** and pleasing God **endures under sorrows** and punishments **when suffering unjustly**, this is no tragedy to be lamented. Rather if they **do good and** yet **suffer** and still **persevere** in goodness, **this *finds* grace with God** and brings His favor. It is the returning good for evil that brings God's blessing, not the suffering itself. **For** (Peter asks half-humorously) **what** far-flung **fame** can they expect **if when** they **sin and are buffeted** with a cuff about the head they patiently endure it? That suffering is no more than they deserve. It is patient endurance of *unjust* suffering that brings the divine reward.

This is a tall order for house-slaves (as it is for all men), so Peter backs up the precept with the inspiration of Christ's example. This endurance of unjust suffering is the very thing to which they **have been called** by Christ. For Peter says, citing Isaiah 53:9, Christ **did no sin, nor was guile found in His mouth**, so that all His suffering was unjustified. Nonetheless, while He was verbally **abused** and reviled by the Sanhedrin at His trial, He **did not counter-abuse**, or respond with insults of His own. While suffering scourging and crucifixion under Pilate, He **did not threaten** them with divine punishment or pronounce God's curse on them. Instead He **delivered Himself over to the One judging righteously**, entrusting Himself to His Father, from whom true justice would eventually come. In all these responses Christ was **leaving behind a model**, that His disciples **may follow after** Him **in His steps**.

The word rendered *model* is the Greek *upogrammos*. It refers to the pattern of letters (Gr. *gramma*) that a school child copies as a way of learning how to write the alphabet. Christ's endurance of unjust suffering thus sets the norm for His disciples. We must not protest when our lives come to imitate His, for this is how we fulfill our discipleship and learn from the Master. His path led to suffering and the Cross, and only after this to the Father's reward. Like one **following after** and stepping in the **steps** and footprints left before us, we must follow Him to His destination of suffering.

Therefore, we should not despise unjust suffering, for it is honorable. Indeed, it was this very thing that worked our salvation. Alluding to Isaiah 53:5 and 12, Peter reminds his hearers that **upon the tree** of the Cross Christ **carried our sins in His body**, and **by His welts** they **were cured**.

The word translated here *carried* is the Greek *anaphero*. In the Greek of Isaiah 53:12, it translates the Hebrew *nasa*, "to lift up, bear, carry," but it is also the usual Greek word to describe lifting up something in sacrifice (compare Ex. 24:5 LXX; Heb. 7:27). The thought is thus that Christ carried away our sins in His own body by offering that body as a sacrifice. **By** the **welts**, wounds, bruises, and stripes He received there, all **were cured** and healed of the affliction of sin and death.

Christ did all this for us that **having departed from the sins** in which we once were held we now **might live to righteousness**. It is this in which our cure and salvation consist. Formerly they were **straying as sheep**, having been deceived and misled by the idols (the word rendered *stray* is the Greek *planoo*, often rendered "to deceive, mislead"; compare Matt. 24:4–5). They had strayed from the right path, wandered into sin, and were helpless as lost sheep before wolves. But now they have **departed from the sins** Christ carried upon the tree and can **live to righteousness**, having returned to the true path. Now they are safe with their true **Shepherd and Bishop of** their **souls** and lives. As **Shepherd** Christ will keep them safe in His sheepfold from their souls' foes in this age and the next. As **Bishop** or Overseer (Gr. *episcopos*), He will rule over them and provide for them. However vulnerable the house-slaves feel before their unjust master, Christ is their true Master, and He will ultimately defend them.

❧ ❧ ❧ ❧ ❧

3 1   Likewise, you wives, submit to your own husbands, that even if any are disobedient to the Word, they may be gained without a word by the conduct of their wives,

2   as they observe your pure conduct in fear.

3   And let not your adornment be external— braiding the hair and putting on gold *jewelry*, or clothing with dresses,

4   but the hidden person of the heart, with the incorruptible *adornment* of the meek and quiet spirit, which is costly before God.

5   For thus formerly the holy women also who hoped in God were adorning themselves, submitting to their own husbands,

6   as Sarah obeyed Abraham, calling him lord, whose children you have become, doing good and not fearing any alarm.

After house-slaves, Peter next turns to wives, since they are to some degree vulnerable to their unbelieving husbands, even as house-slaves are to their masters. All Christians are to submit to the proper authorities (2:13): house-slaves must submit to their masters, and wives must **submit to** their **own husbands**, following their leadership.

It is this shared and universal obligation to submit that connects the house-slaves of 2:18f with the wives of 3:1f, so that Peter says that wives must **likewise** submit to their husbands even as house-slaves submit to their masters. Thus submission is not unique to the spousal relationship, but is a duty common to all Christians. Wives, however, do not submit in the same way slaves do, for the wives, unlike the slaves, submit to their husbands as to their equals. Indeed, Christian wives are co-heirs of the same grace of eternal life as their Christian husbands (3:7).

Theirs is not a cringing servile submission, nor is the submission absolute. Rather, this submission has as its source the wife's **fear** of Christ (Gr. *phobos*; compare its use in 2:17). As said above, Christians are not to fear flesh and blood. Rather, this fear refers to the wife's reverence for Christ, so that she willingly follows her husband's lead as a way of serving the Lord. This, of course, sets limits to her submission, for she would never follow her husband if doing so would contradict her faith in Jesus. Unlike the submission expected of wives in the pagan world (which *was* absolute), the submission of the Christian wife is the submission of one who belongs first and fundamentally to God.

This submission is especially important in cases where the husbands are **disobedient to the Word**. For not all Christian women have Christian husbands, and some pagan husbands object to their wives' religion. (This is another example of the difference between Christian and pagan submission: in the pagan world, the dutiful wife was expected to abandon her religion if her husband demanded it, whereas the Christian wife would never do such a thing.) Peter recognizes that nagging the husband to convert to the Christian faith is not likely to bear fruit. Indeed, it might even be counterproductive, for the husband could say, "Just look what this new faith produces—wives who no longer obey their own husbands! All was perfectly fine in my marriage until the wife heard of this Jesus!"

Peter therefore urges the wives to proper submission, so that even the unbelieving husbands may **be gained** and converted **without**

83

a word as they **observe** the **pure conduct** of their wives. It is seeing a life, not hearing an argument, that will do the trick! And this purity is not confined to sexual chastity, but includes purity of heart as well. It is the entire quality of the woman's life that commends her faith to her spouse.

This is why Peter also urges the wives to **let not** their **adornment be external** only. In the pagan world, women are tempted to obsess about how they look and to let this consume their energies. (This temptation has not faded with time.) Thus they spend hours **braiding the hair**, piling up layer upon layer, **putting on gold** *jewelry* of extraordinary cost, and **clothing** themselves with expensive **dresses**. It is this obsessive excess that is condemned as inconsistent with a life committed to the pursuit of the Kingdom of God (compare Matt. 6:31–33). (Obviously braids and gold are not condemned outright, any more than dresses are, for in denouncing "clothing with dresses," Peter is not counseling nudity.)

Rather, the main focus should be where their true beauty lies— not the external body but **the hidden person of the heart**, the inner person. Outward beauty will one day fade, and no braiding, jewels, or dress can disguise this. The true adornment of the inner person, consisting of a **meek and quiet spirit,** is **incorruptible** and will never fade. Unlike the outward adornments, this inner adornment costs nothing, but even so is **costly** and precious **before God**.

A wife who is inwardly **meek** (Gr. *praus*) is one whose impulses are controlled. The virtue of meekness is not weakness and pathetic self-effacement, but controlled strength; Moses was said to be the meekest man of his time (Num. 12:3 LXX), though he withstood the powerful Pharaoh. Not wives only, but all Christians are urged to this fruit of the Spirit (e.g. Gal. 5:23). A wife is to have a **quiet** (Gr. *esuchios*) spirit as well. This quietness is not total silence, but the inner stillness of those who are at peace. Once again, it is a virtue to which all should aspire, monastics especially (compare the English word "hesychast").

Because of the difficulty of fulfilling this exhortation, St. Peter once again offers an example for inspiration (compare 2:21f). In the same way as the Christian wives are to adorn themselves with a meek and quiet spirit, **the holy women also who hoped in God** as the Christians do **were adorning themselves, submitting to their own husbands**. Thus, for example, Genesis 18:12 says that **Sarah** the matriarch **obeyed Abraham, calling him lord**. The term *lord* (Heb. *adon*; Gr. *kyrios*) in its original context was simply the usual term for husband. Nonetheless, the word did express the subordinate position of the wife, and indicated that Sarah accepted it. Christian wives who hope in God and look for their reward (see 1:13), though formerly pagans, now **have become** Sarah's **children** through their baptism. This presupposes that they continue to live out their baptism, **doing good**, living in submissiveness and good deeds as she did (compare 2:15). In this they need **not fear any alarm** or give way to fear—whatever kind of husbands they have, God will bless them.

ళ ళ ళ ళ ళ

7 You husbands, likewise, co-dwell with *them* according to knowledge, as with a weaker vessel, since she is a woman, and assigning *them* honor as also *being* co-heirs of the grace of life, that your prayers may not be hindered.

Peter then turns to the **husbands**. Though they are not at risk of mistreatment (as house-slaves and wives are), Peter addresses them too, albeit briefly. Because husband and wife form one flesh, it is inconceivable that a Christian exhortation would be addressed to the wife and not to the husband also. Since the gist of the exhortation is that husbands must be considerate of their wives, it is possible that Peter still writes out of concern for the women.

Just as the house-slaves and wives submit, so the husbands must do **likewise** (Gr. *omoios*, the same word used in 3:1 to connect the wife's obligation with the house-slaves'). That is, all Christians must submit to the proper authorities, fearing God and obeying Him (2:13–17). The husbands work out this submission to God by **co-dwelling with** their wives **according to knowledge** and **assigning** *them* honor.

The phrase *according to knowledge* (Gr. *kata gnosin*) probably refers to the husbands' knowledge of God, a usage consistent with other New Testament uses of the term *knowledge* (e.g. 1 Cor. 8:1f; Col. 2:3), and not his knowledge of his wife. That is, the husband's behavior towards the wife must reflect his knowledge of God and His demands, for a Christian husband should live differently from a pagan one.

In particular, the husband must **co-dwell with** his wife **as with a weaker vessel, since she is a woman**. In what does this weakness consist? Surely not in weakness of mind or of character, though ancient pagan opinion said so. Rather, the weakness consists in extra vulnerability, and husbands must respond to this by protecting their wives and caring for them in love.

Also, husbands must **assign** their wives **honor**, since the women are **also co-heirs of the grace of life**. The eternal **life** the husband will inherit on the Last Day will be equally inherited by his wife also, so that they inherit it together as a unity of one flesh—not just as heirs, but as **co-heirs** (Gr. *sugkleronomos*). In the age to come, they will inherit the same Kingdom, and the honor he now gives her recognizes this. If the men refuse to honor their wives in deed and word, God will judge them, and even now their **prayers** will be **hindered** and rejected by God.

☙ ☙ ☙ ☙ ☙

8 Finally, let all be of the same-mind, sympathetic, brotherly-loving, tenderhearted, and humble-minded;

9 not rendering wickedness for wickedness or abuse for abuse, but blessing instead, for you were called for this, that you might inherit blessing.

10 For "let him wanting to love life and see good days stop his tongue from wickedness and his lips from speaking guile,

11 "and let him turn away from wickedness and do good; let him seek peace and pursue it,

> 12 "because the eyes of the Lord *are* upon the righteous and His ears *are open* to their supplication, but the face of the Lord *is* against those doing wickedness."

In summing up his exhortation for all to have proper submission in all their relationships, St. Peter urges **all** to **be of the same-mind, sympathetic, brotherly-loving, tenderhearted, and humble-minded**. Especially during times of persecution, it is easy to become quarrelsome. Peter appeals to his hearers to be **of the same-mind** (Gr. *omophron*), living harmoniously, refusing to argue over trifles. They must be **sympathetic** (Gr. *sumpathes*), caring for others in their sorrows and needs. They should be **brotherly-loving** (Gr. *philadelphos*), treating one another as true family and closest kin. They must be **tenderhearted** (Gr. *eusplagchnos*), with hearts overflowing with compassion, and **humble-minded** (Gr. *tapeinophron*), not disdaining any in the church, but being the servant of all.

Some in the world may persecute them, or verbally abuse them in slander or tongue-lashing. Even so, let them not retaliate, **rendering wickedness for wickedness**, or verbal **abuse for** verbal **abuse**. Let them not try to get their own back or revile in return. Instead, let them respond by **blessing** them. It is **for this** that they **were called** in baptism, that they **might inherit blessing** in the age to come. In baptism they were called to a new life, one in which they will bless others and so be blessed by God in return on the Last Day.

Characteristically, Peter seals his precept by citing the Scriptures. Psalm 34:12–16 also teaches that by blessing our enemies, we inherit blessing on the Last Day. For in that psalm the Psalmist urges the one **wanting to love life and see good days** to **stop his tongue from wickedness and his lips from speaking guile**, so that he **turns away from wickedness** and **does good, seeking peace**.

The word rendered *wickedness* in the Psalm citation in verses 10–11 is the Greek *kakos*, the same word used by Peter in verse 9. Thus Peter portrays the Psalmist as saying that one must not return wickedness, *kakos*, when one encounters it, but **stop his tongue** from speaking it and **turn away** from it. The one who wants **life** and **good days** in the age to come must therefore **do good** even to sinners and **seek peace**, refusing to retaliate.

The Psalmist originally referred to God's blessing of life and good days *in this age*, but Peter applies his words to *the age to come*, for the apostle has no doubt that in this age the Christian will not see good days, but persecution. But the blessing of **life** and **good days** in the age to come is sure, for **the eyes of the Lord *are* upon the righteous and His ears *are* open to their supplication.** He will see how the sinners wickedly use them and will avenge the righteous on the Last Day. Peter's hearers may invoke God's blessing even on those who injure them, for justice will eventually be done. **The face of the Lord *is* against those doing wickedness.** They can rest in the final justice of God.

Suffering from the World

> 𝔰𝔰 𝔰𝔰 𝔰𝔰 𝔰𝔰 𝔰𝔰
>
> 13 And who is there to mistreat you if you become zealots for what is good?
>
> 14 But even if you should suffer for the sake of righteousness, *you are* blessed. And do not fear their fear, neither be shaken,
>
> 15 but sanctify Christ as Lord in your hearts, always prepared for a defense to everyone who asks you for a word about the hope that is in you, but with meekness and fear,
>
> 16 having a good conscience that in *the thing* in which you are spoken against, those assailing your good conduct in Christ may be put to shame.
>
> 17 For *it is* better, if the will of God wills, that you suffer for doing good rather than for doing evil.

In this final part of Peter's exhortations about the Christian's interaction with the world around him, he then deals with the possibility of overt persecution. This part of Peter's exhortation is linked with the previous one by the word **and** at the beginning of verse 13. Citing Psalm 34, Peter urged his hearers to "do good" (v. 11). If they do this and **become zealots for what is good, who is there to mistreat** them? Even pagan society tends to reward good deeds aimed at the public welfare (compare 2:14). They should have nothing to fear from pagan society if they are law-abiding Christians.

But even if they should suffer for the sake of their righteousness and Christian faith, it is still not something to be feared, for they are **blessed**. This blessing refers to the final blessedness of salvation in the age to come, but does not exclude a foretaste of it now. Even now, if they are reproached because of their faith, the Spirit of glory and of God will rest upon them (4:14), filling them with the blessing of God's peace.

Therefore they should **not fear their fear** (that is, fear the intimidating threats of the pagans), **neither be shaken** from their composure in Christ. Instead they should **sanctify Christ as Lord in** their **hearts**. (In speaking of not **fearing their fear** and **sanctifying** the **Lord**, Peter alludes to Is. 8:12–13 LXX. We note in passing that he applies an Old Testament text about the Lord Yahweh as referring to the Lord Christ.) By **sanctifying Christ as Lord**, St. Peter means that the Christian should reverence Christ as the only true Lord from his deepest being, openly confessing Him. (In Jewish thought, martyrs sanctified the Name of God by confessing it in martyrdom.) Society may think Caesar is Lord and ultimately in control, but the believer knows Christ is the One who rules over all, and nothing can befall him that Christ does not allow.

With this unshakable peace, the believer can **always** be **prepared for a defense** of his faith. **To everyone who asks** him **for a word** of explanation **about the hope that is in** him, he can give it and not cower in tongue-tied fear. But let that defense of his faith in the marketplace of daily life be **with meekness** and gentleness. It is always tempting to add to the defense of one's faith a loud assertion of how stupid the other man's faith is. This should be avoided. The defense should also be made with **fear**—that is, with fear towards God, knowing that He hears all our words and will vindicate us at the end.

This presupposes, of course, them **having a good conscience**, and that they are indeed doing good. If they maintain **good conduct in Christ** and live like Christians, in *the thing* in which they **are spoken against** and slandered as evildoers, **those assailing** them will **be put to shame** and proven wrong. For if they do good and **the will of God** (that is, His inscrutable decrees) **wills** that persecution should arise so that they **suffer for doing good**, that is still **better** than if they were **doing evil** and suffered for it. Their decision to keep a good conscience will never be cause for regret, even if by the providence of God it does not result in immunity from persecution.

🍃   🍃   🍃   🍃   🍃

18 For Christ also died for sins once *for all*, the righteous for the unrighteous, that He might bring us to God, having been put to death in the flesh, but made alive in the Spirit,

19 in which also He went *and* heralded to the spirits in prison,

20 who once were disobedient, when the patience of God was waiting in the days of Noah, when the ark was being built, in which a few, that is eight souls were brought safely through water,

21 which corresponding-pattern also now saves you, *namely* baptism—not the removal of filth from the flesh, but an appeal to God for a good conscience—through the resurrection of Jesus Christ,

22 who is at the right *hand* of God, having gone into heaven, angels and authorities and powers having been submitted to Him.

To seal his exhortation to doing good in Christ even if it leads to unjust suffering, St. Peter again brings forward the example of Christ. **Christ also died for sins once *for all*, the righteous** One suffering unjustly **for the unrighteous, that He might bring us**

to God. In the same way, the Christian's unjust suffering is also a pathway to God, and even if he is martyred, it only results in a closer union with Him.

It is the same with Christ—when He was **put to death in the flesh**, He was **made alive in the Spirit**. The contrast here is between the realms of the **flesh** and the **Spirit**: in the realm of the **flesh**, in this visible world, Christ was **put to death**, but in the realm of the **Spirit** and by the Spirit's power, He was **made alive**. In this state, in the days immediately following His death, burial, and resurrection, He **went** and **heralded** His victory **to the spirits in prison, who once were disobedient, when the patience of God was waiting in the days of Noah**. Thus, though death seemed to be an ignominious defeat, it actually led to a light-filled triumph. Likewise, Christians who are martyred will find that death for them also leads to light-filled triumph, for they also will be made alive as Christ was.

Peter's reference to **the spirits in prison** seems to be an allusion to the angelic spirits mentioned in Genesis 6:1–4, who fell into disobedience around the time of Noah's flood. In that passage it says that the sons of God saw that the daughters of men were fair, and they took wives for themselves from among them. This passage has been variously interpreted, but it seems that Peter shares the interpretation current in his day, which is reflected in such works as the Book of Enoch (especially chs. 6—21), written shortly before. In this interpretation, the "sons of God" were angels who lusted after earthly women and fell from their angelic estate. For their sin they were imprisoned until the time of the end, awaiting their final punishment. Peter alludes to this interpretation again in his second epistle, 2:4, as does Jude in Jude 6. Peter mentions here that Christ **heralded** His victory to those spirits in prison because he wants to show that Christ's victory is total and universal. His triumph reaches to the remotest reaches of the cosmos—even over those fallen angels now imprisoned at its farthest ends.

Mention of Noah's flood (the biblical context of the disobedience of the angels) allows Peter to refer to the time **when the ark was being built**, for in it, **a few, that is eight souls** (i.e. Noah, his three sons, his wife and their wives) **were brought safely through**

water. This experience of salvation in the ark foreshadows Christian salvation through baptism (the word rendered *brought safely through* is the Gr. *diasozo*, derived from the word for "saved," *sozo*). Salvation through the waters of the flood is the pattern and type (Gr. *tupos*), and baptism is the **corresponding-pattern** (Gr. *antitupos*), the fulfillment of the foreshadowing. Noah and his family came through the waters to inherit life in the renewed world, and the Christian also comes through the waters of baptism to inherit new life in Christ. For both Noah and the Christian, the life of the old sinful world has been left behind, drowned in the waters. Peter mentions this to show how their **baptism now saves** them and makes them different from the world. Though the Christians be few and outnumbered (even as Noah and his family were **few**), they alone find salvation in this sinful age.

Not, Peter says, that baptism saves automatically. Baptism indeed saves, but not because of the physical act of **removal of filth from the flesh** alone. The baptismal bath alone is not what saves, but rather baptism saves because that bath is also **an appeal to God for a good conscience**. It is the significance of the bath that brings regeneration and salvation; baptism is itself the Church's **appeal** and request to God that the candidate be cleansed in his conscience, receiving the remission of sins. Baptism saves **through the resurrection of Jesus Christ**, for in baptism, the power of the risen Christ enters the life of the one baptized (compare Rom. 6:4–5). Peter mentions this spiritual dimension of baptism to encourage his hearers to continue to walk in the newness of life, maintaining their **good conscience** and blameless life among the pagans. Apart from their righteous life, baptism will not finally avail.

As an encouragement to those suffering, Peter concludes by saying that Jesus Christ is now **at the right *hand* of God, having gone into heaven, angels and authorities and powers having been submitted to Him**. The pagans may think the Christians are a powerless minority with none to plead their cause. It is not so. The Lord of the Christians, Jesus Christ, now rules the cosmos from **the right *hand* of God**, having transcended this world and **gone into heaven** itself. All the spiritual powers of this age—the exalted **angels** and authorities and powers—have been submitted to Him by the Father. Christ rules over all the unseen world, which the pagans think controls the destinies of men. The Christians can persevere in their faith, confident that their Lord will vindicate them at the end.

❧ ❧ ❧ ❧ ❧

4 1 Therefore, since Christ has suffered in the flesh, arm yourselves also with the same insight, because he who has suffered in the flesh has ceased from sin,

2 so as to live the rest of the time in the flesh no longer for the desires of men, but for the will of God.

3 For the time gone by *is* sufficient to have worked out the intention of the Gentiles, having gone on in sensualities, desires, *bouts of* wine-drinking, revels, drinking *parties,* and wanton idolatries,

4 in which they *think it* strange that you do not co-run with *them* into the same flood of dissipation, *and* they blaspheme,

5 who will render a word to Him who is prepared to judge the living and the dead.

6 For *the good news* for this *purpose* has been brought even to those who are dead, that though they are indeed judged like men in the flesh, they may live like God in the Spirit.

Peter continues his exhortation about suffering by urging his hearers to imitate their Lord, if they would be exalted as He was (the **therefore** of 4:1 is a link to the thought of 3:22). **Christ has suffered in the flesh,** and they must **arm** themselves **also with the same insight.** What is this **insight** (Gr. *ennoia,* "point of view, attitude, conception")? It is that the life **in the flesh,** in this world, must inevitably be sacrificed in suffering if one is to do the will of God.

Christ was willing to give up His life to do the will of the Father, and if Peter's hearers had this attitude, it would serve as their armor in their struggle with the world.

That is **because he who has suffered in the flesh has ceased from sin**. The thought here is that Christian suffering sanctifies one's life, separating it from the surrounding worldliness. The connecting concept is that of the flesh: Christ **suffered in the flesh**, and if we **suffer in the flesh**, **the rest of** our **time in the flesh** will **no longer** be lived **for the desires of men, but for the will of God**. The **flesh** (meaning here not so much just the physical body, but rather our life in the world), having been touched by martyric suffering, has been changed. Suffering persecution forces us out of the sinful social network of the Gentiles, so that we run with them no longer.

The concept of **sin** here is not an internal one, but a social one. Peter is not saying that if we suffer persecution, then sinning becomes psychologically and spiritually impossible for us. We can (alas) still quarrel and be lazy and gluttonous. The **sin** Peter has in mind is the life given over to the lusts and **desires of men**, the plans and **intention of the Gentiles**, the whole social network and way of life consumed by pleasure-seeking—in fact the sin referred to in verses 2–4. When we are persecuted, we are out of that network, once and for all.

Peter ironically says that **the time gone by** *is* **sufficient** for such sin anyway. His pagan hearers have spent most of their lives already in such sins—that should be enough for them! And he lists all the things they have **worked out** in their lives and now should leave alone: **sensualities, desires,** *bouts of* **wine-drinking, revels, drinking** *parties***, and wanton idolatries**. The picture is one of many late nights (the nouns are in the plural) spent in drunken orgies and wild parties.

That used to be their life, and their old comrades (the same ones who now **blaspheme** and slander them) *think it* **strange that** they **do not co-run with** them and join them in **the same flood of dissipation**, the same flowing stream of hopeless excess. Their Christian faith has made them so narrow! What's happened? They used to be fun, but now look at them!—them and their stupid god!

Peter exhorts his hearers not to fear slander like this, for those who speak like this **will render a word to Him who is** even now **prepared to judge the living and the dead**. What will these pagans answer when they have to give an account of their sinful lives to the God of the Christians?

Peter drives his point home by saying that *the good news* **for** this *purpose* **has been brought even to those who are dead**. When Christ descended to the land of the dead after His own death, He proclaimed the Gospel to them all, so that all who had pleased God by their righteous lives might go with Him to the Father. (Unlike the verb used in 3:19—"to herald," Gr. *kerusso*, which refers to any heralded proclamation—the verb used here is the Gr. *euaggelizo*, used for preaching the Gospel, the *euaggelion*.)

Thus, though all the dead are **indeed judged like men in the flesh**, the righteous among them may **live like God in the Spirit**. All are **judged like men in the flesh** in that all receive the sentence of death passed on all men in this life (compare Gen. 3:19; Heb. 9:27). But the intent of the Gospel is life, that those who die physically may one day be raised and **live like God,** eternally, **in the realm of the Spirit**, in the age to come. Those of the dead who have lived righteously find the proclamation that Christ has triumphed is indeed good news brought to them, for they are to be rescued from the sentence of death and one day rise to immortal life. The thought here is not of the dead being given a chance to respond to the Gospel and to choose whether or not they will accept it. Rather the thought is of those already saved by their God-oriented lives (see Rom. 2:7) welcoming the good news that rescue is at hand.

Peter mentions this because it underscores Christ's lordship over both the living and the dead. The Christians' God is not some small tribal deity. He is the Lord of all men, both the dead and the living, and all will one day render an account to Him. There is salvation in no one else.

🙐 🙐 🙐 🙐 🙐

7   The end of all things draws near; therefore be restrained and be sober in prayers.

> 8 Before all *things*, have fervent love for one
>   another, because love covers a multitude of sins.
> 9 *Be* hospitable to one another without mur-
>   muring.
> 10 As each one has received a *spiritual* gift, *use* it
>   in serving one another as good stewards of the
>   varied grace of God.
> 11 If anyone speaks, *let him speak* as *it were* the
>   oracles of God; if anyone serves, *let him serve*
>   as by the strength which God supplies; that in
>   all things God may be glorified through Jesus
>   Christ, to whom is the glory and might to the
>   ages of the ages. Amen.

It might seem that the time of judgment will never come, but Peter insists that **the end of all things draws near**. They must **therefore be restrained and be sober in prayers**. The words translated *be restrained* and *be sober* are the Greek *sophroneo* and *nepho*, and they are closely allied. To **be restrained** means to be rational, of sound mind, sensible. Neither persecution nor the thought of the imminent end should cause them to lose their heads. They must also **be sober**, meaning not just that they must not be drunken, but that they must maintain an inner vigilance and balance (compare 1:13, where the same word is used). This inner balance is for the purpose of persevering in their daily **prayers** (Gr. *proseuchas*, a plural), for such prayers are the anchor during these times of stress as the end approaches.

As in the other New Testament references (e.g. Phil. 4:5; James 5:9), this sense of the nearness of the end is not a matter of chronological closeness, but of eschatological imminence. Peter is not predicting that the end will come in a few months or years. He is saying that the end is the next thing on the divine agenda, so that Christians of every age should live in a state of readiness.

Given this, **before all *things*** and of the greatest importance, they must **have fervent love for one another**, living as a community of love in Christ. The hardness of the world might tempt one to become callous and let love grow cold. Love is an action, not a feeling, and believers must take care to continue to care for one another. As an incentive, they should remember that such **love covers a multitude of** their own **sins**, and as they forgive one another, God will forgive them (Matt. 6:14–15).

One way of exhibiting this fervent love is in being **hospitable to one another without murmuring**. Christians in that day were dependent on mutual hospitality when they traveled. In a time when inns were questionable and expensive, most believers opted to stay with other believers. Some would take advantage of this, causing grumbling and complaining. But such abuses of hospitality must not cause them to close their doors. They must maintain hospitality to Christian strangers **without murmuring**.

In their internal life as Christians, each must show love by exercising the *spiritual* **gift** (Gr. *charisma*) given them in such a way as to glorify God. Peter presupposes that upon receiving the Spirit in baptism, **each** baptized believer **received a** *spiritual* **gift**—some function and calling in the body of Christ. It might be dramatic, such as prophecy, or humble, such as giving to the poor (compare Rom. 12:6, 8). Whatever the gift, they are to use it **in serving one another**, for the common good. The gifts do not belong to them. The gifts belong to God, and they are simply administering them **as good stewards of the varied grace of God**. The word rendered *varied* is the Greek *poikilos*. It is usually rendered "various, diverse, manifold," but is also the word used in Genesis 37:3 LXX to describe Joseph's many-colored coat. God's grace is thus varied as the spectrum is varied, for He gives different gifts to each one, according to His will.

These gifted callings are divided between those who **speak** and those who **serve**. Speaking gifts would include such things as prophecy, teaching, exhorting, or counseling (compare Rom. 12:6–8), whereas serving would include such things as healing, giving, showing mercy (compare Rom. 12:8; 1 Cor. 12:9). All are to use their gifts in such a way as to give the glory to God. Thus the one who **speaks** should do so as speaking the words or **oracles of God**, receiving the words from God and acknowledging that they are

His. The one who serves should do so **by the strength which God supplies**, again acknowledging that the power comes from Him. By acknowledging Him in their ministries, **in all things God** will **be glorified through Jesus Christ**, the One in whose Name they have access to God and His gifts. This is only just, for **the glory and might** belong to God **to the ages of ages**. (Like a good Jew, Peter adds an **Amen** to his doxological ascription of glory to God.)

§IV.   Enduring the Fire (4:12—5:11)

Rejoicing in Persecution

ॐ ॐ ॐ ॐ ॐ

12 Beloved, do not *think* strange the burning *ordeal* among you, occurring as a test for you, as *though* a strange *thing* were happening to you;

13 but insofar as you share in the sufferings of Christ, rejoice, that also at the revelation of His glory, you may rejoice, exulting.

14 If you are reproached in the Name of Christ, *you are* blessed, because the Spirit of glory and of God rests upon you.

15 For let not any of you suffer as a murderer, or thief, or evildoer, or as a meddler;

16 but if *any suffer* as a Christian, let him not be ashamed, but let him glorify God in that name,

17 because *it is the appointed* time for the judgment to begin from the House of God, and if *it begins* from us first, what *will be* the end of those not obeying God's good news?

18 And if the righteous is saved with difficulty, where will the godless and sinner appear?

19 Therefore let those suffering indeed according to the will of God commit their souls to a faithful Creator in doing good.

St. Peter begins another major section of his epistle, addressing his hearers as **beloved** (compare 2:11, where he began the last major section in the same way). His hearers have been enduring persecution, which Peter alluded to at the end of the previous section. He now concludes his letter with a series of exhortations on how they are to cope with the fiery trial of living in the world.

When they were pagans, his hearers fit right in with the world around them. Jews might be accustomed to feeling out of step with the secular pagan world, but not these Gentile converts. Feeling out of step is something new for them. They may be tempted to think **the burning *ordeal*** of being ostracized and slandered **strange** and be shaken by it—and may therefore conform more to the pagan world to avoid that ordeal. Peter therefore assures them that their experience is not **a strange *thing* happening** to them, but the normal experience for a Christian, and that it is **occurring as a test**, to purify them.

It is inevitable in this age that the Church should suffer as Christ did (see 2:21). Rather than be shaken, **insofar** as they **share in the sufferings of Christ** they should **rejoice**, because as they share His sufferings, they will share His glory too. **At the revelation of** that **glory** at the Second Coming, they will receive their reward and will **rejoice, exulting** in the triumph Christ shares with them. That final rejoicing therefore should be allowed to spill over into this age, so that they now rejoice in the sufferings that will lead to their final reward. To groan over their sufferings now will lead to disappointment on the Last Day.

Meanwhile, if they are **reproached** because they invoke **the Name of Christ**, they are **blessed**, because even now **the Spirit of glory and of God rests upon** them. The word rendered *rest* is the Greek *anapauo*, used for someone staying and taking his rest (compare its use for the martyrs resting from their labors in Rev. 14:13). The thought here is of the Holy Spirit taking up His abode in a special way in the one who is reviled (compare Stephen's experience in Acts 6:15). He is called **the Spirit of glory and of God** because He bestows a special glory on those on whom He rests, filling them with the power of God, giving a foretaste of the final glory of the age to come. Thus they should not fear the reproach of their neighbors, for it will result in a greater fullness of the Spirit.

Peter, in his insistence on doing good, is clear again that if a Christian is reproached by his neighbors, it must not be because the Christian is **a murderer, or thief, or evildoer** of any other kind. Let the Christians keep the civil laws if they expect to be blessed by God when they suffer! To this short list of crimes (such as being a **murderer** or a **thief**), Peter adds **or a meddler**. This word is difficult to translate. In Greek it is *allotriepiscopos*—literally, one who oversees the things of others. It seems Peter's point here is that Christians should not only not be criminals, they must take care not to be annoying either. For it is possible that Christians may suffer reproach from their neighbors, not because of criminal activity, but simply because they are too irritating in their unwanted rebuke of their pagan friends. Politeness and tact are also Christian virtues!

If anyone does suffer **as a Christian**, however, **let him not be ashamed, but let him glorify God in that name**. The term "Christian," nowadays often a title of honor, was originally a satiric title of insult (like the term "Jesus freak" in the mid-twentieth century). It was coined by the pagans of Antioch, who had a gift for satiric jibe (Acts 11:26). Partisans of Caesar were the *Caesarianoi*, and the partisans of Christ were the *Christianoi*. It is as one of the hated Christians that a follower of Jesus may be denounced by his neighbors. Yet though the term is hurled in his face like a swear word, he ought **not** to **be ashamed** of the epithet, for it contains the holy Name of Christ. Rather, **let him glorify God** that the name is thrown in his face and give thanks that he is able to suffer for his Lord.

For such suffering is inevitable, and it means that it is *the appointed* **time for the judgment to begin** for the children of men. This crisis, wherein men have to choose for or against Jesus Christ, means that the Last Judgment is drawing near and that the ends of the ages have come at last (compare 1 Cor. 10:11). And as in the Old Testament, where God began the judgment by judging and sifting His own People, so it is now. Then judgment began from the sanctuary, the temple (Ezek. 9:6f), and now the final judgment **begins from the House of God**, the Church. The Church is being judged, sifted, and purified **first**, and then it will be the world's turn. For Peter, this is the significance of the persecution in this age—it is God's sifting of His People, testing and purifying them through suffering, the prelude to the final judgment of all. And if the suffering of God's own People is severe, so that **the righteous is saved with difficulty** (i.e. with suffering), **what** *will be* **the end** of **the godless and sinner**, those **not obeying God's good news** of Christ? How much worse suffering is stored up for them at the Last Judgment?

Because of this eschatological ordeal, those who are **suffering indeed according to the will of God** (that is, for their Christian Faith) should **commit their souls** (that is, their lives) **to a faithful Creator**. Their God is the **Creator** of all men and will therefore judge them all. The Christians should entrust their eternal welfare to Him, for He is **faithful** and will keep them for eternal life. And the way to commit themselves to Him is **in doing good**. Their refusal to abandon their integrity in Christ is the way they commit themselves to God's care and judgment.

Exhortation to Unity

> ৯৵ ৯৵ ৯৵ ৯৵ ৯৵
>
> **5** 1 Therefore I, the co-elder and witness of the sufferings of Christ, and sharer also of the glory about to be revealed, exhort the elders among you:
>
> 2 shepherd the flock of God among you, *serving as* bishop not by necessity, but voluntarily, according to God; and not shamefully for gain, but readily;
>
> 3 not as lording it over those allotted *to you*, but being patterns of the flock.
>
> 4 And when the Archshepherd has been revealed, you will receive back the unfading crown of glory.

> 5   Likewise, *you* younger, be submitted to your
>   elders; and all *of you*, clothe yourselves with
>   humility toward one another, for God opposes
>   the arrogant, but gives grace to the humble.

Because of the inevitably of suffering, Peter makes his appeal to the church leaders (the **therefore** of 5:1 connects this appeal to the mention of suffering in 4:19). It was the responsibility of the clergy to care for the believers and prepare them to endure their ordeal. In making this appeal, St. Peter brings forward his personal authority and **exhorts the elders** of the Church as a **co-elder and witness of the sufferings of Christ**, as well as a **sharer of the glory about to be revealed**. That is, he is an elder too, with responsibility for ruling the Church. He is also a **witness of the sufferings of Christ**, one who can attest to the hostilities He endured, which set the pathway for us. He is a **sharer also of the glory about to be revealed** at the Second Coming, so that he awaits that Coming eagerly, as they do.

In this threefold description of himself, Peter places himself in solidarity with his fellow leaders, encouraging them by his personal example as well as by precept. (We note here the great humility of the apostle, who is content to style himself simply as a fellow elder like them, and does not stress his status as leader of the Twelve.)

His appeal to **the elders among** his hearers (that is, to the presbyters, not just to the older men; compare Acts 14:23) is that they should **shepherd** or rule the church with zeal, for it is not their flock ultimately, but **the flock of God**.

Thus they must *serve as* **bishop not by necessity** or compulsion, not serving their brethren with dragging feet, **but voluntarily** and willingly, **according to God**, because He has appointed them to that service. (Reluctance to serve as clergy was all the more likely during times of persecution, when clergy and their families were the first targets.) The Greek verb rendered *serving as bishop* is *episcopeo* (cognate with *episcopos*, "bishop, overseer"). It refers to the elders' ministry of spiritual oversight and pastoral supervision, of watching over the souls of those committed to them (Heb. 13:17). (The terms "elder/*presbuteros*" and "bishop/*episcopos*" were often used interchangeably at that time; see Acts 20:17, 28; Titus 1:5, 7.)

Also, though some remuneration might attach itself to this task, they must **not** do it **shamefully for gain**, as men motivated mostly by money, but **readily**, eagerly, as motivated by the love of God and His people.

Furthermore, they must **not lord it over those allotted** to them, swaggering and insisting on being honored. Instead they must prove themselves **patterns** and examples for **the flock**, walking in humility. Peter doubtless remembers what the Lord said to him on the night on which He was betrayed, that if the disciples wanted to be blessed, they must wash one another's feet (John 13:3–17).

As an incentive, Peter's hearers should remember that **when the Archshepherd**, Jesus (He who is the true Shepherd of their flocks), **has been revealed** at His Second Coming, they **will receive back the unfading crown of glory**. Let them spend themselves for their brethren now, laboring in humility. They will receive their wages soon enough. Crowns of flowers or garlands of leaves are given to victors at the games or to honored citizens. But unlike these crowns, **the crown of glory** Christ gives is **unfading**, like His Kingdom (compare 1:4). It is this reward that He will give to the faithful stewards of His flock. It is Christ, not the children of men, whom the shepherds are truly serving.

After addressing the elders (or presbyters), Peter rounds things off by addressing the **younger** ones. As the leaders have responsibilities to their charges, so **likewise** the younger ones have responsibilities to their **elders**—in particular that of being **submitted** to them and following their leadership. It seems the younger members of the Church are tempted to reject the authority of their leaders (perhaps due to the proverbial impatience of youth?), and Peter urges them to godly submission.

And not just they, but **all** in the Church must **clothe** themselves **with humility toward one another**. The word translated *clothe* is a rare word in Greek, *egkomboomai*, and it is used to describe a vestment that is tied on, such as a servant's apron. All are thus encouraged to put on humility over their other virtues, as an apron is tied on over a tunic. Only thus can they work and stay clean. In their striving for humility and mutual service, they can be encouraged by knowing that **God opposes the arrogant** (who refuse to submit in humility), but He **gives grace to the humble**. If they will gird on humility, God will reward them even now with His grace and favor.

Exhortation to Steadfastness

> ❧ ❧ ❧ ❧ ❧
>
> 6 Be humbled, therefore, under the mighty hand of God, that He may exalt you at the *appointed* time,
>
> 7 throwing all your worry upon Him, because it is a concern to Him about you.
>
> 8 Be sober, keep alert. Your opponent the devil walks as a roaring lion, seeking someone to swallow up,
>
> 9 whom withstand, solid in the faith, knowing that the same sufferings are being accomplished by your brotherhood who are in the world.

Since God gives grace to the humble (v. 5), Peter exhorts his hearers to **be humbled, therefore**, that God **may exalt** them **at the *appointed* time**. This self-humbling refers to their voluntary acceptance of persecution and their refusal to rail against God or abandon Him. If they will do this, God will exalt them at the appointed time of the Last Judgment: now they may be victims, but then they will be victors. This is because their **God**, **under** whose **mighty hand** of providence and judgment they bow, is able to overthrow the kingdoms of men and give the Kingdom to His own people.

This humble acceptance of persecution is no matter of tense teeth-gritting. Rather, they can be serene even in the midst of persecution, **throwing all** their **worry upon** God, **because it is a concern to Him about** them. The image of **throwing** is a vivid one (the Gr. is *epiripto*, used in Luke 19:35 for the disciples throwing their garments upon the donkey on which Christ was to ride), and

Peter here cites Psalm 55:22 LXX. Rather than clutching onto their anxiety over themselves and their families in times of persecution, they can throw it away, giving it to God. He is not indifferent to their pains and sorrows. He who marks the fall of every sparrow (Matt. 10:29) will care for them too.

But God's care for them in this age does not mean they can be careless. Instead they must **be sober** in spirit (Gr. *nepho*, used in 1:13; 4:7) and **keep alert** to spiritual danger. They must be clear-headed and vigilant. For their **opponent the devil walks** about **as a roaring lion, seeking someone to swallow up**. The image is of a lion on the prowl, roaring in hunger, just waiting for an unwary victim to happen by so he can swallow him up in one gulp. Though their pagan neighbors may do the persecuting, their true **opponent** is **the devil**, and he is looking for unwary Christians whose composure persecution might shake into denying Christ, that he might devour them through their apostasy. They must therefore **withstand** the devil, being **solid in the faith**, immovable in their commitment to Christ. The word rendered *withstand* is the Gr. *anthistemi*; it is the word used for Paul's vigorous confrontation of Peter at Antioch (Gal. 2:11). It describes not a passive resistance, but an active opposition. Christians are to **withstand** Satan during times of persecution by boldly confessing Christ before all men, glad to suffer and die for Him.

It will be easier to do this **knowing that the same sufferings are being accomplished by** their **brotherhood**, all the other Christians **who are in the world**. The Christians of Asia Minor are not being singled out or picked on for such treatment. Theirs is the lot of Christians worldwide, the fate of all the disciples of Jesus in this age. They are not alone!

ॐ ॐ ॐ ॐ ॐ

10 Now the God of all grace, who called you into His eternal glory in Christ, after you have suffered for a little *while*, will Himself restore, establish, strengthen, *and* found *you*.

11 To Him *be* might to the ages. Amen.

Peter concludes his exhortation about enduring the fire of living in this age with a final doxology. God is praised because at the end He will be revealed as **the God of all grace**, the One whose ways with His people are all mercy. He **called** them **into His eternal glory in Christ**, calling them in baptism to share Christ's glory in the age to come. Until then, they must **suffer** in this age, but that is only **for a little** *while* compared with the eternal ages in which we will bask in the light of God's love (Eph. 2:7).

After we have suffered throughout this age, God **Himself** (the pronoun is emphatic in the Greek) **will restore, establish, strengthen,** *and* **found** us in His Kingdom. He will **restore** us and mend us (the Gr. is *katartizo*, used in Mark 1:19 for the mending of nets), wiping away every tear from our eyes. He will **establish** and **strengthen** us, nurturing us back to full strength after the exhausting contest of this life. He will **found** us (the Gr. is *themelioo*, cognate with *themelios*, a foundation), making us firm so that we will never be overthrown. No wonder that Peter ascribes all **might** to Him, even to endless **ages**. He is the Almighty, who does whatever He pleases, to the salvation of His own people.

§V. Final Greetings (5:12–14)

ॐ ॐ ॐ ॐ ॐ

12 Through Silvanus, the faithful brother (as I reckon *him*), I have written to you briefly, exhorting and witnessing this to be the true grace of God; stand in *it*!

13 She who is co-chosen in Babylon greets you, and my son Mark *does also*.

14 Greet one another with a kiss of love. Peace *be* to you all who are in Christ.

Having finished his letter, Peter adds a few final greetings. He mentions Paul's friend and companion **Silvanus** (also known as Silas), for it is **through** him that Peter has **written** the epistle, in that Silvanus served as the amanuensis (and possibly the carrier of the epistle too). Since Silvanus had (we suggest) a fair share in the actual wording of the epistle, Peter commends him as **the faithful brother** to assure everyone that he endorses all that was written.

The letter itself is Peter's exhortation and witness to **the true grace of God**. That is, Peter is telling them how to receive God's grace and salvation (viz. by their righteous life and steadfastness of faith). Let them therefore **stand in** it and not be dislodged from the grace in which they now stand.

Peter writes from Rome (styled Babylon for its proverbial sinfulness in Jewish eyes), and he sends greetings from the church there, **she who is co-chosen** along with the churches of Asia Minor to whom he is writing. (Churches were usually referred to in the feminine, since the Church is the Bride of Christ.) Peter's spiritual son Mark sends his greetings too. (Mark was in Rome at that time, and was later to write down Peter's stories of Jesus and publish them as the Gospel of Mark.)

The apostle concludes by bidding them **greet one another with a kiss of love**, the standard Christian greeting of peace that seals their liturgical prayers, for he expects his letter to be read at the liturgical assembly. He adds his own greeting of **peace** to them **all**.

❧ The Second Epistle of St. Peter ❧

Introduction

The Second Epistle of St. Peter represents his last preserved apostolic exhortation before his martyrdom. Some have denied the epistle's authenticity and suggested that Peter did not write this letter. They assert that it was written much later, in Peter's name, and that this practice (of writing pseudonymously, in another's name) was a common and accepted literary convention in the early Church.

This is most improbable, for in fact the practice of writing in the name of an apostle was considered by the Church to be a kind of spiritual forgery, and as claiming an apostolic authority the author did not in fact possess. Thus when a well-meaning presbyter wrote the Acts of Paul and Thecla under Paul's name, he was deposed when the forgery was discovered (Tertullian, *On Baptism*, ch. 17). The Church accepted our epistle because it came to believe it was written by St. Peter. There are other indications also that it was written by St. Peter.

Firstly, the author identifies himself as "Simeon Peter" (not Simon Peter), and this is the same version of his name given in Acts 15:14. It is unlikely that a forger would have the sophistication to reproduce the name by which he was popularly known in this way. A forger would more likely refer to him as "Simon," since this is the name used in the Gospel lists (such as Mark 3:16 and its parallels).

Also, the author claims to have been an eyewitness to the Transfiguration (1:16–18). This cannot be a matter of a later author writing in Peter's name as a literary convention. If this epistle was not written by Peter (or James or John), the author was lying, and it is difficult to see how this could be so in a Christian work.

Again, the author of 2 Peter refers to an earlier letter he wrote (3:1)—obviously a reference to 1 Peter. It is unlikely that a forger would make reference to a former letter, especially since there are no references to it in the rest of the epistle. A forger, if he knew about 1 Peter at all, would have quoted it more freely to make the forgery more convincing. A passing reference is therefore a mark of authenticity.

Finally, there are certain commonalities between 1 Peter and 2 Peter. The author of 2 Peter refers to his hearers as "beloved" (3:1, 8, 14, 17)—just as the author of 1 Peter does (1 Peter 2:11; 4:12). The author of 2 Peter refers to Noah's flood, mentioning that there were eight souls aboard the ark, just as the author of 1 Peter does (2 Peter 2:5; 1 Peter 3:20). These common unreflective references point to the same author, for it is unlikely that a forger would possess the sophisticated subtlety to reproduce them from the earlier letter.

We may therefore be confident that the epistle was indeed the work of Peter. Certainly the Church has come to value it as the words of the big fisherman and prince of the apostles.

Peter probably arrived in Rome in the summer of 63, after the release and departure of St. Paul. It was, we suggested, in the following winter or spring that he wrote his first epistle. The Great Fire of Rome occurred in July of 64, sparking a persecution of the Christians of Rome in the months following.

It seems that Peter knew he would be arrested and executed in the persecution that began after the Fire of Rome, and that he wrote this second epistle as a final testament, probably in the spring of 65. He saw that the churches to whom he wrote his first epistle were being menaced by false teachers, and he wrote to warn them of the threat before his imminent death.

Who were these false teachers and what did they teach? It seems they denied that Christ was returning, and they lived lives of sexual license and self-indulgence, basing their libertinism on certain phrases found in the letters of Paul (e.g. "All things are lawful for me"; compare 1 Cor. 6:12). They seem to have interpreted the stories of Jesus according to their own myths and ideas, as well as all the Old Testament Scriptures (much like the later gnostics). Peter heard that these teachers were infiltrating the ranks of the Church and wrote to warn the churches of their influence.

He wrote to remind the Church to cling to its apostolic foundations in a time when a flood of heresy had begun to inundate the faithful. In our own age, when that flood has not yet abated, Peter's final word to the Church loses none of its urgency.

❧ The Second Epistle of St. Peter ❧

§I.   Opening Greeting (1:1–2)

🙠 🙠 🙠 🙠 🙠

1 1   Simeon Peter, a slave and apostle of Jesus
Christ, to those who have been allotted an
equally-precious faith with us, by the righteousness of our God and Savior, Jesus Christ,

2   Grace and peace be multiplied to you in the
real-knowledge of God and Jesus our Lord,

The author begins by identifying himself as **Simeon Peter**, this
being a Semitic version of his name (rather than the un-Semitic
Simon) and a confirmation of the letter's authenticity. (A Gentile
forger would not know to use the Semitic version of his name.) Peter
describes himself as the **slave** of Jesus Christ, indicating his total
submission to Christ's Lordship, as well as His **apostle**, with authority to teach. He addresses his hearers (probably the same Gentile
Christians to which he sent his first letter) as **those who have been
allotted an equally-precious faith with us, by the righteousness
of our God and Savior, Jesus Christ**.

The word rendered *allotted* is the Greek *laxchano*, which literally
means "received by lot" (compare its use in Luke 1:9; John 19:24,
where lots were cast); the thought here is of the Gentiles receiving
their own portion from God. Though they are Gentiles, Peter is
insistent that theirs is **an equally-precious faith with** that of his
fellow Jews, and that the Gentiles are no second-class Christians. This
was the point he made in 1 Peter (e.g. 2:9–10) and in his ministry
(compare Acts 10:34–35). This **faith** and inclusion in the People

of God is the result of **the righteousness of** their **God and Savior, Jesus Christ**. (We note in passing this reference to the deity of Jesus.) The term *righteousness* is here used for Christ's kindness and love, just as it is used for God's kindness and love in Psalm 145:7 LXX. It is through the Lord's grace that the Gentiles have been called, and Peter writes with a keen awareness of their dignity in Christ.

In bidding them **grace and peace** (the standard opening for letters), Peter writes that such will **be multiplied** to them **in the real-knowledge of God and Jesus our Lord**. It is as they grow in intimate knowledge of **God** as revealed through **Jesus** the **Lord** (i.e. not just knowledge, Gr. *gnosis*, but **real-knowledge**, Gr. *epignosis*) that the blessing of God wished for them in the greeting will be realized. Peter thus uses the literary conventions of letter-writing to teach them of the necessity for growth in holiness.

§II.   True Knowledge of God (1:3–11)

True Knowledge Promotes Godliness

ᴔ ᴔ ᴔ ᴔ ᴔ

3 *seeing* as everything for life and piety His divine power has given us through the real-knowledge of Him who called us by His own glory and virtue.

4 Through these He has given us the precious and great promises, that through these you might become sharers of the divine nature, having fled from the corruption that is in the world by desire.

Peter continues his sentence from verse 2, anxious as he is to encourage his hearers in the true-knowledge of God. He mentioned the real-knowledge of God and Christ in verse 2, and he now in verse 3 hastens to say that such **real-knowledge** was given them when they were baptized. (The verb *call* here is in the aorist tense and refers to their baptism.) Peter affirms that **everything** necessary for **life**

and piety His divine power has given us Christians **through the real-knowledge** of Christ (and not through any gnostic lore).

The reference seems to be to the **divine power** of the Holy Spirit given in baptism, when Christ **called us** to Himself and made us His disciples, for it is by the Spirit that we receive life and the power to live a pious and godly life (compare Rom. 6:4; 8:2). Christ **called us** to Himself by **His own glory and virtue**. That is, the Christians converted to Christ and accepted baptism because they saw in Christ the **glory** of God and the **virtue** and moral beauty that ravishes the spirit of man. The Christ proclaimed in the Gospel reached out and captured their hearts, so that they loved Him without ever seeing Him (compare 1 Peter 1:8).

It is **through these** (that is, through Christ's glory and virtue) that **He has given us the precious and great promises**. What promises? The **promises** that He will come again and glorify us, bestowing eternal life and incorruption (see John 5:28–29; 6:40; 11:25–26; 14:3). When Christ manifested His **glory** and **virtue** throughout His ministry, He promised over again that He would judge the world and that His own disciples would share the glory He would reveal (see 1 Peter 5:1). When Christ returns and fulfills these promises, we will **become sharers of the divine nature**. The glorified Christ is incorruptible, and we shall be made incorruptible; death now has no dominion over Him, and one day it will have no dominion over us (1 Cor. 15:53). Thus the incorruptible nature of divinity will then be bestowed on us by grace. (This does not deny that even now we share a foretaste of that divine nature as we are transformed into His glorious image; 2 Cor. 3:18).

All of this presupposes, of course, that we will have successfully **fled from the corruption that is in the world by desire** and lust. In order to share the divine immortality in the age to come, we must not lose ourselves in the moral corruption and lust of this age.

꤮ ꤮ ꤮ ꤮ ꤮

5   And for this very *reason* also, having brought
     to bear all diligence, in your faith supply virtue,
     and in virtue, knowledge;

6   and in knowledge, self-control, and in self-control, perseverance, and in perseverance, piety,

7   and in piety, brotherly-love, and in brotherly-love, love.

8   For if these are existing in you and are increasing, they appoint you neither idle nor unfruitful in the real-knowledge of our Lord Jesus Christ.

9   For he with whom these are not present is blind, shortsighted, having forgotten his cleansing from his old sins.

10 Therefore, brothers, be all the more diligent to make your calling and choice confirmed, for doing these things, you will never once trip;

11 for thus will be richly supplied to you the entrance into the eternal Kingdom of our Lord and Savior Jesus Christ.

For this very *reason* (that is, because they must escape the moral pollution of this age to be saved), they must strive with all **diligence** and eagerness **in** their **faith** to **supply virtue** and moral excellence. (The word rendered *virtue*, Gr. *arete*, is the same one used to describe Christ's moral beauty in v. 3.) Merely having **faith**, or baptismal assent to joining Christ, is not enough. A life of godliness must be added to it in abundance (the word translated *supply* is the Gr. *epichoregeo*, meaning not just to supply but to supply *abundantly*).

To encourage his hearers in their striving for godliness, Peter lists eight virtues (the number of perfection in the ancient world). It is significant that the list begins with **faith** and ends with **love**, for love is the crown of all the virtues. The order in which they come is not, however, otherwise significant. (Peter is not saying, for example, that one should not supply self-control until one has acquired knowledge.) Godliness is one, and cannot be parceled out programmatically. Rather, Peter simply exhorts his hearers to the classic virtues with which they were familiar from the philosophers.

Thus, in their **virtue** and moral excellence, they must have

knowledge (Gr. *gnosis*) or discernment, the ability to perceive the true way. They must have **self-control** (Gr. *egkratia*) and be able to resist the sensuality of the world. They must have **perseverance** (Gr. *upomone*) and be able to endure the long night of temptation. In addition, they must have **piety** (Gr. *eusebeia*; the same word used in 1:3), the godliness that separates them from the world. They must have **brotherly-love** (Gr. *philadelphia*), warmhearted affection and loyalty to their Christian brethren. And finally, they must have **love** (Gr. *agape*), a self-sacrificing benevolence to all men. In producing this list, Peter has one eye on the false teachers against whom he writes to warn his hearers, for they have none of these qualities.

In urging his hearers to godliness, Peter assures them that if these qualities **are existing** in them (Gr. *uparcho*, a strong verb) and **are increasing**, this will **appoint** them **neither idle nor unfruitful in the real-knowledge of our Lord Jesus Christ**, which real-knowledge is the focus of their baptism (compare Col. 3:10). The experience of Christ that began when they were born again is to work in the world and bear fruit, as they do good in society (see 1 Peter 2:15). Growth in these virtues will assure them of this.

On the other hand, if **these** virtues are **not present** at all in them, they have obviously **forgotten** their baptismal **cleansing from** the **old sins** of their pre-Christian days. Baptism is illumination and bestowal of spiritual sight, but they have become **blind** and **short-sighted**. The pairing of the word *blind* with the word *shortsighted* is unusual, for the latter is not as strong as the former. The thought here seems to be that those who have refused to grow in holiness are now spiritually blind, in that they cannot see what is right in front of them—namely, what Christ has done for them in cleansing their sins. The reference to being *shortsighted* (Gr. *muopazon*; compare the English "myopic") indicts them for their present inability to perceive truths they once were able to see clearly.

Therefore, because of this danger, they must **be all the more diligent** and eager **to make** their **calling and choice confirmed** and steady. The words *calling* and *choice* refer to Christ's calling them in baptism to be His disciples, and His choosing them from out of the world. (The word *choice* is often translated here as "election.")

Peter says that if they will pursue virtue vigorously, this will make their status as Christ's disciples the more sure, so that they **will never once trip** or fall into apostasy. In this way they **will be richly supplied** (the word rendered *supplied* is again the Gr. *epichoregeo*, for an abundant supply) with an **entrance into the eternal Kingdom**. That is, they will not only enter the Kingdom, but will be **richly** rewarded upon their arrival.

Apostolic Witness to True Knowledge

ॐ ॐ ॐ ॐ ॐ

12 Therefore, I will intend always to remind you about these things, even though you know *them*, and have been established in the present truth.

13 And I regard *it* as righteous, as long as I am in this tabernacle, to rouse you by a reminder,

14 knowing that the removal of my tabernacle is imminent, even as our Lord Jesus Christ has made plain to me.

15 And I will also be diligent to make you have these things in memory at any time after my exodus.

St. Peter then comes to the main purpose of his epistle, which is **to rouse** his hearers **by a reminder** of the necessity for godliness, and to warn them against the dangers of popular false teaching. He is not teaching newfangled precepts, but tried and true ones, things that they **know** and **have been established in**. He **regards** *it* as only **righteous**, as his duty before God, to constantly remind them, both now in this letter and until the end. He does this all the more so since he **knows** that **the removal of** his **tabernacle is imminent**. (By *tabernacle* Peter means the temporary tent of his body in which he dwells as he sojourns on this earth.) He knows that his death will occur soon, probably because (as we have suggested) the persecution following the Great Fire of Rome has begun by this time, and his arrest and martyrdom are only a matter of time. This is **even as our**

Lord Jesus Christ has made plain to him, for He told His apostle that he was to glorify God through martyrdom (John 21:18–19).

As they were urged to "be diligent" (v. 10), so Peter intends **also** to **be diligent** in such reminders, so that his hearers may **have these things in memory at any time after** his **exodus** from this life.

ৡৡ ৡৡ ৡৡ ৡৡ ৡৡ

16 For we did not follow after sophistically-made myths when we made known to you the power and coming of our Lord Jesus Christ, but we became observers of that One's greatness.

17 For when He received honor and glory from God the Father, such a voice as this was brought to Him by the Majestic Glory: "This is My beloved Son with whom I *Myself* am well-pleased,"

18 and this voice we *ourselves* heard brought from heaven when we were with Him on the holy mountain.

In reminding them of the glory to come when they enter the eternal Kingdom and partake of the divine nature in the resurrection (1:4, 11), Peter emphasizes the truthfulness of this hope. His opponents, the false teachers, deny such an eschatological hope (3:3–4), possibly saying these things are fairy tales worthy only of children, and that the only resurrection is the spiritual resurrection experienced in baptism, which is already past (compare 2 Tim. 2:18).

Peter rebuts these denials. Unlike his opponents with their myths (compare 1 Tim. 1:4; Titus 1:14), he and the other apostles **did not follow after sophistically-made myths**. When they **made known** to the church **the power and coming of our Lord Jesus Christ**, this was no myth, but sober historical fact, for they **became observers** of the Lord's **greatness**. The word rendered *made known* (Gr. *gnorizo*) is something of a technical term for revealing a mystery; and the word translated *observer* (Gr. *epoptes*) is the usual word designating one initiated into a mystery, an eyewitness to hidden secrets. By using these terms, Peter stresses that the apostles are transmitting truths given directly by God.

The content of the apostolic preaching is **the power and coming of our Lord Jesus Christ**. The apostles preach that Christ will come again to judge the world and to reward His people, and this future Second Coming is the very thing Peter's opponents are denying. Thus Peter responds by saying that this hope is not a myth, but rather that the apostles beheld that future glory with their own eyes.

This occurred at the Transfiguration, **when** Jesus **received honor and glory from God the Father** (Matt. 17:1f). There Jesus shone with the radiance of the Father, and a **voice was brought to Him by the Majestic Glory** (like a good Jew, Peter uses this circumlocution when referring to God manifesting Himself), saying, **"This is My beloved Son with whom I** *Myself* **am well pleased."** Peter stresses that, as true eyewitnesses, they (the Greek pronoun is emphatic) **heard this voice**, the Voice of God Himself, **brought from heaven when** they **were with** Christ there. The place of the Transfiguration Peter calls **the holy mountain**, to stress that God truly appeared there. (Compare the appearance of God in the burning bush, which thereby made that spot holy; Ex. 3:5.) Peter and the other apostles truly witnessed Christ's **greatness** and glory.

This, Peter says, proves the reality of the Second Coming, for Christ Himself pointed to the Transfiguration as a foretaste and proof of His future glory at the Coming (Matt. 16:28). The **greatness** He will manifest at the Second Coming was **observed** by the apostles at His Transfiguration. The apostles thus can confidently proclaim the reality of His Coming because they themselves have *seen its glory already*.

ॐ ॐ ॐ ॐ ॐ

19 And we have the prophetic word *made* more-confirmed, to which you do well to pay attention, as to a lamp shining in a murky place, until the day dawns and the light-bearer arises in your hearts.

20 But know this first, that every prophecy of

> Scripture is not of one's own explanation,
> 21 for a prophecy was not ever brought by the will
> of man, but men brought by the Holy Spirit
> spoke from God.

Not only that, but they **have the prophetic word**, the Old Testament Scriptures, *made* **more-confirmed**. The Scriptures are **more-confirmed** because they are in the process of being fulfilled. Formerly, the prophecies of the glory of the Messiah were all in the future. Now, they are coming true before their very eyes (such as in the Transfiguration), and this confirms even more their truthfulness. St. Peter urges his hearers to **pay attention** to the Scriptures, studying them and feeding their hopes upon them. In the dark and **murky place** of this age, the Scriptures are **a lamp shining**, giving them light and direction (Ps. 119:105). This is the only light available in the night of this age. At the Second Coming, **the day** will **dawn** and **the light-bearer**, Jesus, the Morning Star (compare Rev. 22:16), will **arise in** their **hearts** to banish all doubt and fill them with His light. Until that blessed day, the Scriptures are their source of hope.

But they must be careful. The false teachers love to twist the Scriptures, interpreting them according to their own particular ideas (3:16). The Christians must therefore **know this first** of all, that **every prophecy of Scripture is not of one's own explanation**. The nonapostolic interpretations of these teachers are to be soundly rejected, for these men are untaught and unstable, devoid of the Spirit (3:16; Jude 19). The Scriptures must be interpreted by men in whom is the Spirit, the apostles and their successors (which interpretations are preserved now in the Tradition of the Church). This is consistent with the origin of the Scriptures themselves, for **a prophecy was not ever brought by the will of man** (as his own private ideas), **but men brought** and carried along **by the Holy Spirit spoke from God**. The prophecies (such as those declaring the glory of the Lord and His future Coming) were given entirely by the Spirit, and cannot be interpreted by those devoid of the Spirit—such as the false teachers.

121

§III.   **False Teachers Promote Ungodliness (2:1–22)**

ॐ ॐ ॐ ॐ ॐ

2 1 But there were false-prophets also among
          the people, as there will also be false-teachers
          among you, who will sneak in destructive fac-
          tions, even denying the Master who bought
          them, bringing imminent destruction upon
          themselves.

      2 And many will follow after their sensuality, and
          because of them the way of the truth will be
          blasphemed;

      3 and in their greed they will buy you with
          fabricated words; their judgment of old is not
          idle, and their destruction does not become
          drowsy.

In warning his hearers of the necessity of godliness, Peter then
warns them of an increasing threat to that godly walk—the rise
among them of **false-teachers**. Just as **there were false-prophets
among** Israel of old, tempting them to apostasy, so **there will also
be false-teachers** in the Church who oppose the work of God. As
in ancient times, when the false prophets opposed the work of the
true prophets, the Enemy still raises up lies as an alternative to the
truth. Though the false teachers are even now among them (see
v. 13), Peter speaks of them coming in the future (**there will be
false-teachers**) because they will come in greater and greater
abundance.

Who were these false teachers? It is impossible to speak with
certainty. They seem to have been Christian teachers who were now
mixing worldly theosophical ideas into their Christian teaching to
form a syncretistic gnostic brand of Christianity. With these new
ideas, they drew disciples to themselves, functioning as gurus in a
cult of personality. Their lifestyles were characterized by **sensuality** and sexual immorality (probably involving their new female

disciples), and by **greed** (probably collecting fees for their teaching). It is apparent that they denied the Second Coming and twisted both the Old Testament Scriptures and the letters of Paul in support of their new ideas and their licentious lifestyle (3:15–16). It is possible they considered their authority as superior to that of the angels, asserting that the angelic hierarchies were inferior to them. They were still calling themselves Christian teachers and mixing with the rank and file believers at the gatherings of the Church, using those gatherings to collect more disciples of their own.

Peter warns his hearers that these men are no longer true Christians at all, and that the **factions** (Gr. *airesis*, "sect," sometimes rendered "heresy") they are creating and **sneaking in** are **destructive**. Though they once belonged to Christ, by pursuing their own way they are now in effect **even denying the Master who bought them** with His Blood. Their **sensuality** and licentious living will entice **many** (so that the Christian **way** they claim to follow **will be blasphemed** and maligned by thoughtful men, and the Church will lose credibility in the world's eyes). **In their greed** for money and pleasure, **they will buy** their disciples **with fabricated words** (Gr. *plastos*; compare our English "plastic"), exploiting the unwary by telling them what they want to hear.

Though they seem to prosper, their **destructive factions** will **bring imminent destruction upon themselves**. This **judgment** from God was set **of old**, as God long ago decreed wrath upon the ungodly (compare Jude 4), and even now this judgment is **not idle**. Indeed the **destruction** awaiting them **does not become drowsy** (Gr. *nustazo*; compare its use in Matt. 25:5); though it may seem to tarry and sleep, it waits vigilantly for them and will surely find them at the end.

🦋 🦋 🦋 🦋 🦋

4 For if God did not spare sinning angels, but cast *them into* Tartarus and delivered them up to pits of gloom, kept for judgment;

5 and did not spare the ancient world, but guarded the eighth *man in the ark*, Noah, a

---

> herald of righteousness, when He brought a flood upon the world of the impious;
>
> 6 and He condemned the cities of Sodom and Gomorrah to destruction, *reducing them* to ashes, having made them an example to those intending to *live* impiously,
>
> 7 and He rescued righteous Lot, oppressed by the sensual conduct of unprincipled *men*,
>
> 8 (for by what he saw and heard, *that* righteous man, while dwelling among them, had his righteous soul tormented day by day by their lawless works),
>
> 9 then the Lord knows *how* to rescue the pious from testing, and keep the unrighteous under punishment for the day of judgment,
>
> 10 and especially those who go after the flesh in polluting desire and despise dominion.

That this is so may be seen by examining God's way with the righteous and the unrighteous in Scripture. Peter produces three examples.

First, he calls attention to the **sinning angels**, the sons of God mentioned in Genesis 6:1–4. Even though they were mighty angels, God did **not spare** them when they indulged in such perverse sexuality, **but cast *them into* Tartarus and delivered them up to pits of gloom**. The word translated *cast into Tartarus* is the Greek *tartaroo*. Peter here uses classic Greek terminology to express the Hebrew concept of the fallen spirits of Genesis 6 being imprisoned until the end. For the Greeks, **Tartarus** was the underground abyss deeper than Hades, deeper than the land of the dead, the place where rebellious gods were imprisoned. It was here that the fallen angels were judged and **kept for judgment**.

Secondly, Peter says that neither did God spare the entire **ancient world** when it sinned also, but **brought a flood upon the world of the impious** (Gen. 6—9). He did, however, guard **the eighth *man* in the ark**, Noah, for he was **a herald of righteousness**, and strove (albeit unsuccessfully) to bring those around him to repentance. In saying that Noah was **the eighth** *man*, Peter not only means there were seven others with him in the ark. He probably also alludes to eight as the number of perfection, saying thereby that Noah was blameless in his time (Gen. 6:9).

Finally, Peter says that God **condemned to destruction** two whole cities, **the cities of Sodom and Gomorrah**, *reducing them to ashes*, making them forever after **an example to those intending to** *live* **impiously** in sexual immorality as they did (Gen. 19). As He saved righteous Noah from the midst of the wicked, so He **rescued righteous Lot** from their midst also, since Lot was **oppressed by the sensual conduct** of his neighbors.

These examples are very carefully chosen. Both the fallen angels and the men of Sodom and Gomorrah were involved in sexual immorality—just as the false teachers are. And in the judgments that came upon the ancient world and upon the cities of Sodom and Gomorrah, God saved those who were committed to righteousness (Noah is called **a herald of righteousness**, and Lot is described as **righteous** three times in two verses)—just as Christians are called to be righteous in the face of such sensuality.

These examples mean that **the Lord knows** *how* **to rescue the pious from testing**, helping them to emerge victorious from the temptation to sin. They also mean that the Lord knows how to **keep the unrighteous under punishment for the day of judgment**, so that sinners will not escape the judgment of God. God's just sentence will eventually be carried out—both upon the sinning angels and the sinning men. Given all this, the Christians should resist the temptations to unrighteousness and remain pious, knowing how God will deal with the pious and the unrighteous—**especially** the unrighteous like the false teachers, who **go after the flesh in polluting desire** of lust, **and despise dominion**.

ॐ ॐ ॐ ॐ ॐ

10 Daring, self-willed, they do not tremble when
   they blaspheme glories,
11 whereas angels who are greater in strength and

---

power do not bring a blaspheming judgment against them before the Lord.

12 But these, like irrational animals, born by nature for capture and destruction, blaspheming in *matters* they are ignorant of, will in the destruction of them indeed be destroyed,

13 *suffering* wrong as a reward of wrong. They regard indulgence in the day as a pleasure. *They are* stains and blemishes, indulging in their deceits as they co-feast with you,

14 having eyes full of an adulteress, and unceasingly *looking for* sin, luring unstable souls, having a heart trained in greed, cursed children,

15 leaving behind the straight way they have gone astray, having followed after the way of Balaam, the *son* of Bosor, who loved the reward of unrighteousness,

16 but he had a reproof of his own violation; a mute donkey, expounding in a man's voice, hindered the prophet's derangement.

Peter continues his denunciation of the false teachers to warn the faithful away from them. He described them in verse 10a as sexually immoral and as those who "despise dominion." The word rendered *dominion* is the Greek *kuriotes*. It is used to describe the angels by Paul (Eph. 1:21; Col. 1:26) as well as by the author of the Book of Enoch (61:10). That is probably how Peter uses the term here, given that he deals with themes contained in the Book of Enoch (e.g. fallen angels imprisoned in Tartarus). The false teachers despise these angelic orders and **do not tremble when they blaspheme** those **glories**. This just shows how impiously **daring** and **self-willed** they are, for the **angels** themselves, even though they are **greater in strength and power** than the false teachers, **do not bring a blaspheming judgment against them before the Lord**. The false teachers, though men, do not hesitate to slander the angels, but the angels, though greater than men, do not slander them before God, nor bring any reviling condemnation. (Compare Jude 9, which says that the Archangel Michael would not bring a condemning judgment even against the devil, but left the judgment to the Lord.)

How do the false teachers blaspheme the angels? Probably not by actually cursing them, just as they do not deny their Master by actually saying, "I deny Jesus" (2:1). In speaking both of their denials and their blaspheming, Peter is giving his interpretation of the significance of their actions. In the first case, Peter says their heretical self-aggrandizing means they are in effect denying Jesus as their true Master. In the case of them reviling the angels, I suggest that Peter is also giving his interpretation of their actions. What they are actually doing, possibly, is asserting that they are superior to the angels, with an intimate knowledge of God's mysteries superior to theirs, and that even the high celestial orders are inferior to them. That, St. Peter says, is blasphemy against the angels. It is in this sense that the later gnostic heretic Menander blasphemed, for he claimed a magical power strong enough to overcome the angels (reported by St. Irenaeus in his *Against Heresies*, 1, 23, 5).

Far from being superior to the angels, the false teachers are really lower than men; they are **like irrational animals**. Some animals are **born by nature for capture and destruction**, dangerous brutes and creatures of instinct, to be hunted down and destroyed. These men are always **blaspheming in *matters* they are ignorant of** (such as the celestial glories), courting the divine judgment, and they will **indeed be destroyed** just like those dangerous brutes. This will be fitting, for they will suffer **wrong as a reward of** doing **wrong**.

Not only are they daringly blasphemous, they are patently impious too. **They regard indulgence** and reveling **as a pleasure**, even **in the day** (though even other libertines had the decency to wait for the evening). They are **stains and blemishes** in the church. The gatherings of the Christians are meant to be stainless sacrifices of praise, but the presence of these men mars everything, even as blemishes disqualify sacrificial offerings. As they **co-feast with** other

Christians in their *agape* fellowship meals, they go about **indulging in their deceits**, looking to take in the unwary. Their **eyes** are **full of an adulteress, unceasingly** *looking for* **sin, luring unstable souls**. Each woman they meet they regard as a potential adulteress, and they are always on the hunt for the vulnerable. (The verb rendered *luring*, Gr. *deleazo*, comes from the world of hunting and fishing.) Their **hearts** are **trained in greed**, in an ever-increasing desire for more. Just as training in the gymnasium makes one strong (the word rendered *trained* is the Gr. *gumnazo*, from which the English word "gymnasium" is derived), so these men are strong in getting what they want, coolly efficient experts in acquisition. As such, they are **cursed children**, a brood under the curse of God, spreading that curse to all they catch.

They have **left behind the straight way** for another way, **the way of Balaam** (Num. 22—24), a famous false prophet who **loved the reward of unrighteousness** and was hired to curse Israel for money. In the Old Testament story, his name is given as "the son of Beor," not **the** *son* **of Bosor**. Peter, however, is not here making a mistake. Rather, he is making a very Jewish play on words, for in Hebrew the word for "flesh" is the word *basar*. Peter is saying that Balaam was a son of the flesh, not of the Spirit, a false prophet, not a true one.

And Balaam **had a reproof of his own violation** of God's Law—**a mute donkey, expounding** like a prophet **in a man's voice, hindered the prophet's derangement** and stopped his folly. (Peter here makes another play on words in the Greek: Balaam's animal reproved his *paranomia* [*violation*] and hindered his *paraphronia* [*derangement*].)

The word used to describe the donkey's sound (translated *expound*) is the Greek *phtheggomai*, used for loud proclamations; the related word *apophtheggomai* is used for the utterances of holy men and prophets. The thought here is that Balaam was so irrational in his lust for money that even his own donkey was more of a prophet than he was. In their greed, the false teachers are every bit as deranged as he.

ॐ ॐ ॐ ॐ ॐ

17 These are waterless fountain-*fed wells* and mists driven by a storm, for whom the gloom of darkness has been kept.

18 For expounding swollen *words* of uselessness, they lure by desires of the flesh, in sensuality, those who are scarcely fleeing from those who live in deception,

19 promising them freedom while they themselves are slaves of destruction, for by whom anyone has succumbed, by this one he is enslaved.

20 For if after they have fled from the pollutions of the world by the real-knowledge of the Lord and Savior Jesus Christ, they are again entangled in them and succumb, the last *state* has become worse for them *than* the first.

21 For it would be better for them not to have really-known the way of righteousness, than having really-known *it*, to have returned from the holy commandment delivered to them.

22 *It has* occurred to them *according to* the true figure, "A dog returns to its own vomit," and "A sow, having washed, *returns* to rolling in the mire."

The apostle continues his impassioned denunciation. These men are **waterless fountain-*fed wells***. People go to a well, for its presence promises life-giving water. In the same way, the faithful may go to these teachers who promise spiritual life. But they will find the promises hollow, for they have no life to give, and the **fountain-*fed well*** is **waterless** and empty.

Also, they are **mists driven by a storm**. Just as the haze is easily dispersed by a sharp wind, so these men are ephemeral, and they and their teaching will not last. Soon they will be gone, and the **gloom of darkness** waits to receive them.

They **expound** (Gr. *phtheggomai*; compare v. 16) **swollen *words* of uselessness**, using these to **lure** their victims **by desires of the flesh, in sensuality**. They spout their vaunted and exaggerated claims, which are actually useless when it comes to giving life. Using sex as the bait, they take in **those who are scarcely fleeing from those who live in deception**. That is, they seduce the vulnerable recent converts, ones who are still in the process of breaking with their immoral pagan past. With their vaunted claims, they **promise freedom** from sin, **while they themselves are slaves of destruction** and spiritual corruption (Gr. *phthora*, the same word used in v. 12). The false teachers have succumbed to sin and so are in no position to grant victory over it to others. The sensuality they practice with their disciples reveals their own helplessness.

Let potential converts, then, avoid those offering such freedom! (Verses 20–22 refer probably to the converts, rather than to the teachers, for the same verb *apopheugo*, "flee from," is used in both v. 18 and v. 20.) For **if after** these new converts **have fled from the pollutions of the world by the real-knowledge of the Lord** (Gr. *epignosis*, see 1:2–3, 8), **they are again entangled in them and succumb** along with their new teachers, **the last *state* has become worse for them *than* the first**. The judgment awaiting them as apostates will be worse than if they were merely pagans. Thus **it would be better for them not to have really-known** (Gr. *epiginosko*) **the way of righteousness** at all, than to have found life in Christ and then **to have returned** to their sin **from the holy commandment**, the apostolic tradition, **delivered to them**. (The word translated *delivered* is the Gr. *paradidomi*, cognate with *paradosis*, "tradition.")

Joining the false teachers may seem, therefore, like a bold new move, an entry into exciting deeper truths. But in reality it is just a tragic return to the old ways of sin from which they only too recently emerged. No great fulfillment awaits them, but only the degradation of vomit and mire. They will find the **true figure** and proverb fulfilled in their experience: **"A dog returns to its own vomit,"** and **"A sow, having washed, *returns* to rolling in the mire."** (The first figure is from Prov. 26:11; the second from the *Story of Ahikar*, current in that day.) If they **return** to sin from the holy commandment as a dog **returns** to its own vomit and a sow to its mud, they simply prove that they are dogs and sows, for the outward behavior reveals the inner nature. Thralldom to these teachers reveals a brutal and pagan heart still beating within their outwardly Christian breast.

§IV.   Though False Teachers Scoff, Wait for the Lord's Coming (3:1–18)

❧ ❧ ❧ ❧ ❧

3 1   This *is* now, beloved, the second epistle I am writing to you in which I am rousing your sincere mind by a reminder,

2   that you may remember the words foretold by the holy prophets and the commandment of the Lord and Savior by your apostles.

3   Know this first, that in the last days mockers will come with mocking, going according to their own desires,

4   and saying, "Where is the promise of His Coming? For since the fathers slept, all *things* remain on thus from the beginning of creation."

5   For in maintaining this, it escapes *them* that by the word of God the heavens existed long ago and the earth was held-together from water and through water,

6   through which the world then *existing* was destroyed, being flooded with water.

7   But the present heavens and earth by the same word are being treasured up for fire, kept for the day of judgment and destruction of impious men.

Peter now returns to warning the faithful, addressing them as **beloved**, his usual form of address when beginning a new section (compare 1 Peter 2:11; 4:12). He writes to **rouse** their **mind by a**

reminder that they must be holy; because their **mind** and attitude is **sincere** and pure, they will heed his reminder. He underscores the importance of this reminder by saying that this is **the second epistle** he has written to them about it, for his first one also contained many exhortations to godly living (compare 1 Peter 1:13f, which uses the same word for *mind*, Gr. *dianoia*).

These exhortations to godliness and judgments on impiety are contained in **the words foretold by the holy prophets** (hence the importance of the prophetic word; 1:19), as well as in **the commandment of the Lord and Savior** as transmitted **by your apostles**. Peter here speaks of the apostles as **your apostles**, referring to the particular apostles who reached his hearers, for different apostles reached different groups. The thought here is that the apostles can be trusted because they are *your* apostles (unlike the false teachers, who have no claim on your loyalty). Both the prophets (in the Scriptures) and the apostles (passing on Christ's words) gave the same exhortation to godly living, and so it can be trusted—let them abide by it!

In striving for godly living, they must **know this** as of **first** importance, that **mockers will come with mocking, and saying, "Where is the promise of His Coming?"** That is, if they would retain their incentive to holiness, they must be forewarned against the cynical scoffers who will deny the Second Coming and the final judgment. These scoffers are not seeking to serve God and truth, but are **going** about simply to satisfy their **own desires** and lusts. These men are a sign that **the last days** have come, for the last days (that is, the entire era from the Day of Pentecost onwards; see Acts 2:16–17) are to be characterized by the presence of spiritual opposition to God's work (compare 1 John 2:18). Their argument is that **since the fathers slept** (that is, since the Old Testament patriarchs died), **all *things* remain on thus from the beginning of creation.** In their view, nothing has ever changed in history since the beginning of the world—and so it never will. The world continues in unbroken stability and will never end. The thought is in keeping with paganism, which assumes the eternity of the cosmos.

In reply, St. Peter says that **in maintaining this, it escapes *them*** that by the word of God the heavens existed long ago and the earth was held-together from water and through water. That is, in asserting that the earth is eternal, they forget that it was created, and that the act of creation is already an example of breaking the existing stability of nonexistence. Creation *ex nihilo* is in itself an example of God's intervention. In Genesis 1:1–10, **God** by His creative **word** created the cosmos, forming the earth **from water and through water**. These verses declare that prior to the creation of the earth there was only the primordial deep, with the Spirit of God moving on the face of the waters (Gen. 1:2), so that the world was created **through water** (i.e. through the instrumentality of this primordial sea). The earth was also created **from water**, in that the dry land appeared after the waters were gathered together in one place (Gen. 1:9).

Furthermore, water, which is the agent and matrix of creation, is also the agent of destruction, for the world came to be **destroyed, being flooded with water**. St. Peter stresses this to show that water can only cause the destruction of the world through the intervention of God. Water in itself is not harmful to the world, for it is the agent of its creation. Rather, God intervened to disrupt the stability of the world after it was created, judging with a flood all those who lived on it. Thus, the scoffers cannot maintain that all continues as it has since the beginning of the world or that the world is subject only to natural causes.

This being the case, the past history of the world is no argument against the fiery judgment of the Second Coming. **The present heavens and earth**, **by the same word** of judgment that sentenced it once before to a judgment of water, are **being treasured up** and reserved for a judgment of **fire**.

---

৯৯ ৯৯ ৯৯ ৯৯ ৯৯

8   But do not let this one *fact* escape you, beloved, that with the Lord one day *is* as a thousand years, and a thousand years as one day.

9   The Lord is not slow about His promise, as some regard slowness, but is patient toward

---

> you, not intending that any perish, but for all
> to reach repentance.
> 10 But the Day of the Lord will come as a thief, in
> which the heavens will pass away with a roar,
> and the elements will be destroyed, burning
> *up*, and the earth and the works in it will be
> found.

Peter again addresses his hearers as **beloved**, beginning a new section. Though certain truths have escaped the scoffers (v. 5), his hearers must not let a certain crucial truth **escape** *them*. Namely, **that with the Lord one day** *is* **as a thousand years, and a thousand years as one day**. Peter here alludes to Psalm 90:4, saying that with God **a thousand years** is **as one day**, for He is not bound by time as we are, and with Him **one day** *is* **as a thousand years**. That is, He does not measure time as we do. He has an intensity we do not (being able to do in one day the work of a thousand years), and a perspective we do not (so that a thousand years' passing does not wear out His purposes any more than does that of one day). Thus our human impatience is a poor measure with which to judge God's designs.

The mockers may say that Christ's Coming is overdue and seek to sow doubt about whether He is coming at all. But the faithful must be forewarned against such. That Christ has not yet returned does not mean that **the Lord is slow about His promise** to return (**as some**, such as the scoffers, **regard slowness** and measure divine Providence). His delay does not mean that He will not fulfill His promise. Rather it means that He **is patient toward** His world, **not intending that any perish, but for all to reach repentance**. He is slow to judge because He is merciful; His delay is to give men time to repent and be saved. Rather than using the time elapsing before the Coming as an argument to blaspheme, the mockers ought to be using it to repent!

For **the Day of the Lord will come** at last—and suddenly, unexpectedly by the world, **as a thief** (for thieves do not preannounce their arrival). In that Day, **the heavens will pass away with a** crackling **roar** as from a firestorm, **and the elements will be destroyed, burning** *up* with the Presence of God. The cosmos, down to its very building blocks (its **elements**, Gr. *stoichea*), will be dissolved—there will be no place to run, none to hide. On that day, **the earth and the works in it** (that is, all of us) **will be found**. All of our works will become manifest, and all our secrets known. Let all repent now, for His sudden return will allow no time for repentance then.

இ இ இ இ இ

11 Since all these things are being destroyed thus, what kind of *persons* ought you to be, in holy conducts and pieties,

12 expecting and hurrying the coming of the Day of God, because of which the heavens will be destroyed, being *set* on fire, and the elements, burning up, will melt.

13 But according to His promise we are expecting new heavens and a new earth, in which righteousness dwells.

Peter once again stresses his main point: **Since all these things are being destroyed thus, what kind of** *persons* **ought** they **to be, in holy conducts and pieties**? (The plural for *conducts* and *pieties* probably refers to individual acts of holiness and charity on the part of the believers.) The Coming of the Lord to judge the world means that they ought to continue in godliness, resisting the sensual temptations of false teachers. Far from believing the mocking of the false teachers about the Coming of the Lord never occurring, they must persevere in **expecting** this **coming of the Day of God** and His triumph, and even **hurrying** it.

In what sense do the Christians **hurry** the Second Coming? Here we face an insoluble mystery, for the plans of the eternal God are not open to the puny wisdoms of men. But it does seem as if God in some measure sovereignly hears our prayers, when we pray in the Our Father, "Thy Kingdom come," and the holiness undergirding those prayers is not forgotten by the God who sees the beginning from the end. We are to expect that Day with joy, yearning for it eagerly, because even though it means that the very **elements** of the cosmos, **burning up, will melt**, yet **according to His promise we are expecting new heavens and a new earth** in its place. For He not only promised to come (vv. 4, 9), He also promised joy in the new age. In the new cosmos He will bring in place of the old, **righteousness** will **dwell**. The word rendered *dwell* is the Greek *katoikeo*, used for people dwelling and settling down at home in the land. In this world, righteousness is a stranger, but in the age to come, it will find its true home.

🦋 🦋 🦋 🦋 🦋

14 Therefore, beloved, since you expect these *things*, be diligent to be found by Him stainless and blameless, in peace,

15 and regard the patience of our Lord *as* salvation, just as also our beloved brother Paul, according to the wisdom given to him, wrote to you,

16 as also in all *his* epistles, speaking in them about these *things*, in which are some things difficult to understand, which the untaught and unstable twist, as *they do* also the rest of the Scriptures, to their own destruction.

As Peter comes to the end of his epistle, he again addresses them as **beloved**, summing up his teaching. As they expect the Coming of the Lord, let them **be diligent to be found by Him stainless and blameless** when He comes, and **in peace**. The words rendered *stainless* and *blameless* (Gr. *aspiloi* and *amometoi*) denote the opposites of the false teachers, who were earlier described as "stains and blemishes" (Gr. *spiloi* and *momoi*). That is, the faithful must keep themselves from the sinful lifestyles characterizing the world (and exemplified by the false teachers), and live **in** undisturbed holy **peace**. That is, they must **regard the patience of our Lord** and His delay *as* **salvation**, giving the world time to repent and be saved, and must not give heed to the arguments of the immoral scoffers.

As confirmation of his exhortation to perseverance in godliness, Peter concludes by appealing to his **beloved brother Paul**, who **wrote** to them **according to the wisdom given to him**. Peter is writing from Rome and is aware of Paul's considerable literary output. (Perhaps Peter's hearers have read Paul's circular letter to the Ephesians.) Let them heed Peter's message, for Paul, whom everyone knows, says the same **in all *his* epistles**. It is not right to oppose Paul's teaching to his own.

Peter admits that in these epistles there are **some things difficult to understand, which the untaught and unstable twist, as *they do* also the rest of the Scriptures**. That is, these false teachers twist Paul's teaching even as they twist the Old Testament Scriptures. In what way they twist Paul's writings, we do not know. Perhaps they misuse his words, "All things are lawful for me" (see 1 Cor. 6:12), to support their immoral behavior. Perhaps they misuse his saying about being raised up with Christ (Col. 3:1) to support their view that the resurrection is already past, and that a physical resurrection at the Second Coming is not to be expected. Certainly they are adept at twisting his words.

The word rendered *twist* is the Greek *strebloo*, used for wrenching in torture. The false teachers and gnostics deal with any authoritative writings as they will, reading their own improbable myths into them, in utter disregard of the apostolic interpretations. Such interpretations lead only **to their own destruction**.

Finally, we note that when Peter refers to Paul's writings and **the rest of the Scriptures**, he is not asserting here that Paul's epistles are part of the Scriptures—that assertion from the Church will come later. Peter only means that both Paul's writings and the Old Testament Scriptures share the same fate in the hands of the false teachers.

ঔ৾   ঔ৾   ঔ৾   ঔ৾   ঔ৾

17 You *yourselves* therefore, beloved, knowing *this* before, guard yourselves lest, being carried-off by the deception of unprincipled *men*, you fall from your own stability,

> **18** but grow in the grace and knowledge of our
> Lord and Savior Jesus Christ. To Him *be* the
> glory, both now and to the day of eternity.*

* *The final "Amen" was probably added by a later scribe to Peter's original doxology.*

St. Peter ends (with a final **beloved**) telling them they now **know before** all the strategies of those opposed to God. They are forewarned and forearmed, and may now **guard** themselves, so that they may not **be carried-off by the deception** of the heretics. In the apostolic tradition transmitted to them, they have all the **stability** they need—let them not **fall from** it! Instead, let them **grow in the grace and knowledge of our Lord and Savior Jesus Christ**. Being rooted in that tradition and rejecting the fables of the heretics does not mean stagnation. God called them to **grow** and become strong and mature as they come to know and experience Christ. He is the source of their growth and salvation—and **to Him *be* the glory, both now and to the day of eternity**.

Peter ends his epistle (and his life) on this note of praise, giving glory to Jesus Christ. The apostle's eyes are on this age, but also on the age to come, and his desire is to glorify his Lord both now and in eternity.

❧ The Epistle of St. Jude ❧

Introduction

As Christians have sorted through the treasures of the New Testament writings, it has been easy to undervalue the Epistle of Jude, for it is very short (a mere 25 verses) and was not written by a great apostle such as Peter, John, or even James, the first bishop of Jerusalem. But in a collection of crown jewels, all the jewels are to be valued, and we should not fail to appreciate this small but radiant literary gem.

It was written by Jude (that is, Judah, Gr. *Judas*), the brother of James, and therefore the "brother" of the Lord. The Lord's "brothers" (or kin) are mentioned in Matthew 13:55 as "James and Joseph, Simon and Judas," and it is this last who is the author of this epistle. Like James, he does not stress his family relation to Christ, for such things are spiritually irrelevant. Just as James describes himself simply as "a slave of God and of the Lord Jesus Christ" (James 1:1), so Jude also describes himself simply as "a slave of Jesus Christ" (Jude 1). For both James and Jude, what matters is the wisdom they have to impart, not their genealogical lineage.

Jude does, however, add that he is the "brother of James." This is significant, and perhaps reveals some of the circumstances of his writing. James wrote with great authority as the bishop of the mother church in Jerusalem, and his death left something of a void.

The church historian Eusebius reports "a firm tradition" that "after the martyrdom of James and the capture of Jerusalem [i.e. after AD 70], those of the apostles and disciples of the Lord who were still alive assembled from all parts, together with those who, humanly speaking, were kinsmen of the Lord, for most of them were still living. Then they all discussed together whom they should choose as a worthy person to succeed James, and voted unanimously that

Simeon, son of Clopas, was a worthy person to occupy the throne of the Jerusalem see" (*Church History*, 3, 11).

I would suggest that Jude, as the Lord's brother, wrote this epistle in the late 60s or early 70s, after James's death and prior to this apostolic meeting mentioned by Eusebius. By then, a number of other apostles (such as Peter and Paul) had died, and their living witness had begun receding into history.

Jude came to be aware of an urgent problem menacing the churches nearby in the form of false teachers. He had no doubt seen Peter's epistle dealing with this issue and wanted to add his own voice to help counteract this spreading problem. Jude's epistle was therefore a tract, hastily but carefully written to begin to deal with this crisis. He mentions in his opening greeting that he is the brother of James to claim for himself something of James's authority.

The actual addressees are impossible to determine with certainty. They seem to have been Gentiles. They were troubled by false teachers, and the characteristics of these teachers mentioned by Jude lead one to suspect that perhaps they were not unrelated to those denounced by Peter in his second epistle. The church in Jerusalem had close ties with the church in Antioch (compare Acts 11:22, 27f), and it is possible that Jude wrote this letter as a circular to a number of churches, sending it first to those in Antioch, who began to be vexed by the same problems that had vexed the churches in the surrounding area, which churches Peter had written to.

Scholars have long noted the similarity of the epistles of Jude and 2 Peter. But though they both use the same images and vocabulary, it is rare that they use exactly the same phrases and wording. It certainly appears, however, as if one author made use of the other. As mentioned above, I suggest that Jude had seen the Second Epistle of Peter and made use of it in his hastily written tract. He did not quote it exactly or copy out its phrases, but rather had it in mind when he began writing. This would explain both the similarity of images and the lack of verbal identity.

❧ The Epistle of St. Jude ❧

§I.   Opening Greeting (1–2)

❧ ❧ ❧ ❧ ❧

1   Jude, a slave of Jesus Christ *and* brother of
    James, to those who are called, beloved by God
    the Father, and kept for Jesus Christ;
2   May mercy and peace and love *be* multiplied
    to you.

As with the other epistles of the New Testament, Jude does not
just begin his letter with the required, "A writes to B; greetings."
Rather, he expands the opening greeting to convey theological
truth.

Though he is a kinsman of Jesus, Jude still describes himself
as the **slave of Jesus Christ**, for concerns of kinship do not matter in the Kingdom. What matters is his service to Christ, whom
he serves as his absolute Master. Jude also describes himself as the
brother of James, since (as mentioned in the above introduction)
he is appealing to James's authority as the well-known leader of the
Jerusalem church.

He writes **to those** whom God **called** to Himself through holy
baptism. Despite being Gentiles (as we have suggested), they are
beloved by God the Father and **kept** safe through their faith **for
Jesus Christ**, who will gather them into His Kingdom at His Second
Coming. The actual location of these addressees cannot be known
for sure, but we have suggested the city of Antioch as a possible
location. The letter was probably written as a circular letter, to be
sent to a number of locations, beginning from Antioch.

Jude wishes for **mercy and peace and love** to be **multiplied** for his hearers as gifts from God. As will be apparent from the letter following, these gifts will only come to them as they cling to the faith and avoid the threat from false teachers.

§II.   Urgent Warning Against False Teachers (3–19)

ళ్ళ ళ్ళ ళ్ళ ళ్ళ ళ్ళ

3   Beloved, while I was making all diligence to write you about our common salvation, I had the necessity to write to you exhorting *you* to contend for the faith which was once *for all* delivered to the saints.

4   For certain men have slipped in, those who were written-before of old for this judgment, impious *men* who change the grace of our God into sensuality and deny our only Master and Lord, Jesus Christ.

Jude begins by telling his hearers of the urgency of his letter. For all his zeal against heretics, he is a man of tender heart and exhorts his hearers as **beloved** (compare also vv. 17, 20). Indeed, it is his love for them that provokes his wrath against the heretics, for these imperil his beloved fellow Christians.

In his urgency, Jude says that he was **making all diligence**, every effort, **to write** to them about their **common salvation**, but news of the threat of false teachers has pressed upon him the **necessity** to write about this instead. We cannot know what the content of Jude's originally planned letter about their **common salvation** was to be (possibly a series of moral exhortations, such as in the Epistle of James?). But if they hearken to the false teachers, they will fall away from that salvation, and the originally planned letter will be pointless. So it is that Jude feels compelled to write a different letter, one in which he **exhorts** them to **contend for the faith which was once *for all* delivered to the saints**. This last phrase contains a number of important words.

The word rendered *contend* is the Greek *epagonizomai* (a

compound of *agonizomai*, which means "to engage in athletic contest, to fight, to race"; compare John 18:36; 1 Cor. 9:25; 1 Tim. 6:12). The compound *epagonizomai* speaks of a strenuous effort, an all-out fight to counter error and preserve the faith. That **faith** is the apostolic tradition, and it was **once *for all* delivered to the saints**. The word rendered *once for all* is the Greek *apax* (compare its use in Heb. 9:28 to describe the final and definitive sacrifice of Christ). This shows that the faith is not something gradually revealed over time (so that the false teachers might claim to be revealing it). Rather, it was given in its entirety in the past, through the apostles, and can neither be added to nor subtracted from. It was delivered to the saints (i.e. to the rank-and-file believers, not to any secret elite). The word translated *delivered* is the Greek *paradidomi*, cognate with *paradosis*, "tradition." This faith comes to us as tradition, something transmitted from the past and to be handed on. Tradition is not something to be feared; it is the means by which the saving faith comes to us.

This pugnacious tenacity to tradition is essential because **certain men have slipped in** among them. They were **written-before of old for this judgment** that Jude will describe. The written traditions of Israel (such as the Book of Enoch, to be quoted in vv. 14f) long ago pronounced God's judgment upon the **impious**, and no one should be shaken (or seduced) by the presence of their novel teaching. Though these men may preach **the grace of God**, their understanding of it is such as to **change** it **into sensuality**. For they engage in immoral sexual practices, and seek to justify them by appealing to God's grace and their supposed spiritual freedom. As they gather their own disciples in a self-serving cult of personality, they thereby **deny** the **only** true **Master and Lord, Jesus Christ**. Let all avoid these men!

ॐ ॐ ॐ ॐ ॐ

5   Now I intend to remind you, though you know
     all things once *for all*, that the Lord, after saving
     a people from the land of Egypt, in the second
     place destroyed those who did not believe.
6   And angels who did not keep their own

---

domain, but left their own dwelling, He has kept in eternal bonds under darkness for the judgment of the great day.

7 As Sodom and Gomorrah and the cities around them, since they in like manner as these fornicated out and went after different flesh, are laid before *us* as an example in undergoing the penalty of eternal fire.

8 Likewise notwithstanding, these dreaming ones also defile the flesh, and reject dominions and blaspheme glories.

9 But Michael the archangel, when he disputed with the devil and discussed about the body of Moses, did not dare to bring against him a blaspheming judgment, but said, "The Lord rebuke you."

10 But these ones blaspheme the things they do not know, and the things they understand by nature, as irrational animals, by these things they are destroyed.

Jude tells his hearers that being baptized is not enough to save them—they must persevere in godly living too. He stresses that, though he is telling them these things, he is not (as the false teachers do) imparting new teaching. Rather, they **know all things once for all** (Gr. *apax*; compare v. 3). He is not adding to the deposit of the faith, simply **reminding** them of what they already know. In confirmation of this exhortation, he adduces three examples.

First of all, he reminds them that **the Lord, after saving a people from the land of Egypt,** afterwards **destroyed those who did not believe** (Num. 14). Those Israelites liberated by God in the Exodus were the model and paradigm of salvation. Nevertheless, those who did **not believe** (Gr. *pisteuo*), but rejected the faith (Gr. *pistis*) revealed on Mount Sinai, were destroyed by God. Being once saved by God was not enough; they had to persevere in that faith.

Secondly, Jude refers to the **angels who did not keep their**

own domain, but left their own dwelling to sin with women on earth (Gen. 6:1–4). These God has **kept in eternal bonds under darkness for the judgment of the great day.** Even though they were exalted angels, this was not enough to save them after they had sinned against God. The angels apostatized in that they left their own place and did not keep within the bounds set for them. Since they did **not keep** (Gr. *tereo*) their own place of light, God **kept** them (Gr. *tereo*) in a place of **darkness**.

Finally, Jude refers to **Sodom and Gomorrah and the cities around them** (Gen. 19), **since they in like manner as these** angels who sinned sexually also **fornicated out and went after different flesh.** The word rendered *fornicated out* is the Greek *ekporneuo*; it is a more intensive form of the verb *porneuo*, "to fornicate," and here is used to describe gross immorality, **going after different flesh** (i.e. "strange flesh," denoting homosexual relations). These cities **are laid before** all **as an example** of how God will judge such sexual sins, for they were burned up, **undergoing the penalty of eternal fire,** the fire of God from heaven, so that the land still smoldered and remained barren—a warning of the eternal fire of Gehenna that awaits the false teachers.

Jude chooses these examples from Scripture very carefully, for false teachers **likewise** sin, **notwithstanding** these terrifying examples. Like the children of Israel after the Exodus and like the fallen angels, they have apostatized from their former faith and from God. Like the fallen angels and like Sodom and Gomorrah, they indulge in sexual sins (quite possibly including homosexual sins, which were rampant in that Gentile culture, since Jude makes a point of speaking of **different flesh**).

St. Jude describes those teachers as **dreaming ones.** This is because they cite their dreams as the justification for their teachings and practices, regarding these dreams as divine revelations and visions (compare Col. 2:18). Despite these claims to superior revelation, they **defile the flesh** with sexual immorality (even as the sinning angels and the cities of Sodom also did), as well as **reject dominions and blaspheme glories.** This refers to their claim, probably based on their dreams, to be superior to the angels, the **glories** in the heavens

145

(often called *dominions*; see Eph. 1:21; Col. 1:26). (See commentary on 2 Peter 2:10f.) These claims are considered to be insulting to the angels and blasphemous.

Such pride compares unfavorably to the attitude of the angels themselves. Alluding to a story told in a Jewish apocalypse, *The Assumption of Moses*, Jude tells of how **Michael the archangel, when he disputed with the devil and discussed about the body of Moses, did not dare to bring against him a blaspheming judgment, but said, "The Lord rebuke you."** In this story, Michael, the angelic defender of Israel, was **disputing with the devil** after Moses had died. The devil, the accuser, said that **the body of Moses** should not be buried, since Moses had committed murder in Egypt (Ex. 2:12). Michael did **not bring** against Satan **a blaspheming judgment**, or revile him, but simply said, **"The Lord rebuke you,"** leaving him to the judgment of God.

The contrast between Michael and the false teachers is stark. These men insult the angels, but the chief angel himself, though immeasurably greater than any man, did not even insult the devil. The humility of the angels shows up the strutting pride of the false teachers as the pathetic sham it is. **These ones** persist in **blaspheming** angels, claiming to be experts in **things they do not know** anything about. The things they *do* **understand by nature**, instinctively, are their lusts and sexual practices, the things they share with **irrational animals**. And it is by indulging in **these things** that they are **destroyed** in God's final judgment.

🪰 🪰 🪰 🪰 🪰

11 Woe to them! For they have gone in the way of
    Cain, and for reward they have been poured out
    in the deception of Balaam and been destroyed
    in the contradiction of Korah.

Jude continues his denunciation like a prophet of old, pronouncing a doom of **woe** upon the false teachers. He begins his denunciation with a series of three doomed men: Cain, Balaam, and Korah.

The false teachers have **gone in the way of Cain** (Gen. 4), choosing a path that leads far from God, even as Cain did. Cain is cited here not as a murderer, but as an example of someone who deliberately chose evil over good. In the Targum (the Aramaic paraphrase of the Hebrew text) of this story, Cain says, "There is no judgment, no Judge, no future life." If the false teachers Jude denounces are similar to those denounced in 2 Peter, the reference to Cain is apt, for these men also deny the Second Coming and final judgment.

The false teachers **for reward have been poured out in the deception of Balaam** (Num. 22—24). The image of them being **poured out** is one of rushing headlong, as in an unstoppable stream. These heretics, drawn to **reward** and financial gain, have rushed into **the deception** and error **of Balaam**, the famous false prophet. For the sake of money, they have opposed God and His purposes, even as Balaam did.

Finally, the false teachers have been **destroyed in the contradiction of Korah**. (We can see a progression of action here: they went down a certain way, rushed headlong down in a mad hurry, only to be destroyed at the road's end.) The **contradiction of Korah** was the rebellion he mounted against Moses when he defiantly opposed his authority (Num. 16). He and all his supporters perished when the earth opened up to swallow them alive. The false teachers are opposing the authority of the apostles, and a terrible doom awaits them too. (The aorist tense—*been destroyed*—is used to show the certainty of their doom.)

ॐ ॐ ॐ ॐ ॐ

12 These ones are those who are hidden reefs in your love-feasts when they co-feast with you fearlessly, shepherding themselves, waterless clouds, carried along by winds; fruitless late-autumn trees, doubly dead, uprooted;

13 wild waves of the sea, foaming out their own shame; straying stars for whom the gloom of darkness has been kept forever.

Jude continues his earnest denunciation, using images from the sea, air, land, and the heavens. He is not just giving vent to his spleen, but speaking as a watchman of the Church, warning the flock of the dangers of following these men.

They are **hidden reefs**. Just as unseen reefs in the sea pose a danger of shipwreck to ships, so these men are a danger to the souls of the faithful. The false teachers **co-feast** with the rank and file **in** their **love-feasts** and fellowship meals, using those occasions to **fearlessly** and brazenly draw disciples after them. Though they claim to be shepherds and pastors, in reality they are only **shepherding** and caring for **themselves**, for they care nothing for the flock.

Also, they are **waterless clouds, carried along by winds**. Clouds bearing rain are a much-needed blessing, but these men have nothing to give (see Prov. 25:14). As clouds are driven by winds, so these men are unsubstantial and will soon be driven away into oblivion.

They are **fruitless late-autumn trees**. The image here is of trees that should have borne fruit but did not, and so by late autumn (past the season for fruit-bearing) none can be expected, for they are dead. So these men also are spiritually dead, incapable of giving life by their teaching. Indeed, they are **doubly-dead**, even as barren trees that have been **uprooted**, and thus doubly incapable of bearing fruit.

They are **waves of the sea**, restless for evil, constantly producing shameful deeds, just as the sea is constantly **foaming out** and tossing up filth and flotsam on the shore (Is. 57:20).

Finally, they are **straying stars for whom the gloom of darkness has been kept forever**. (The word rendered *straying* is the Greek *planoo*, cognate with *plane*, "deception," in v. 11.) Falling stars may look sensational as they light up the night, but they are soon gone, embraced by the darkness of night. These men are straying from the path of truth, and the gloom of darkness of hell has been reserved for them. Their straying path will end in Gehenna.

ॐ ॐ ॐ ॐ ॐ

14 And to these also Enoch, the seventh from Adam, prophesied, saying, "Behold, the

> Lord came with myriads of His holy ones,
> 15 to do judgment against all, and to reprove every soul about all their impious works, which they impiously did, and about all the hard things which impious sinners have spoken against Him."
> 16 These are grumblers, blamers, going according to their own desires; their mouths speak swollen *words*, marveling at faces for the sake of *gaining* profit.

The appearance of such men should not alarm any of the faithful. Their rise was long ago foreseen as part of the end-time opposition to God. Jude quotes from the Book of Enoch 1:9 as an example of how their rise and doom has been long expected: when **the Lord** finally **comes** (at the Second Coming) **with myriads of His holy** angels, He will **do judgment against all, and reprove every** single **soul about all their impious works, which they impiously did, and about all the hard** and blasphemous accusations **which impious sinners have spoken against Him**. The doom of impious sinners is sure.

These impious sinners are the **grumblers**, the **blamers**, the very false teachers who are vexing the churches. In calling them **grumblers** and **blamers** or fault-finders, Jude aligns them with the rebellious Israelites who grumbled at God in the wilderness and experienced His wrath (Ex. 16:9; Num. 16:41). The false teachers, in rebelling against the apostolic tradition, are rebelling against God Himself. Their rebellion is seen in their behavior. They go about **according to their own desires** and lusts among the unwary, their **mouths speaking swollen** *words* of self-aggrandizing claims (the phrase is reminiscent of the blasphemies of God's foe, the Little Horn, found in Dan. 7:20; 11:36). They go about **marveling at faces for the sake of** *gaining* **profit**, feigning admiring amazement at people's reactions ("How perceptive you are to recognize my wisdom!"). They are masters at flattering people in order to gain advantage and win them over.

ॐ ॐ ॐ ॐ ॐ

17 But you, beloved, ought to remember the words that were spoken before by the apostles of our Lord Jesus Christ,

18 that they were saying to you, "In the last time there will be mockers, going according to their own impious desires."

19 These are the ones who cause divisions, soulish, not having the Spirit.

Despite the slick flattery of these men, Jude's hearers will be able to resist them if they will but **remember the words that were spoken before by the apostles of our Lord Jesus Christ, that they were saying to you, "In the last time there will be mockers, going according to their own impious desires**." Jude refers to the predictions of the apostles as a group, and how they warned that false teachers would arise (see for example Acts 20:28–32), but he expresses their teaching in the words of 2 Peter 3:3 (which, we suggest, he had read before writing his own epistle). Jude does not quote Peter word for word, but the similarity is too striking to be coincidental.

The faithful, therefore, expecting mockers to come who will follow their own impious desires and lusts, can easily recognize the flatterers among them as the self-serving scoffers predicted by all the apostles.

Jude concludes his denunciation of the false teachers by saying that they are **the ones who cause divisions**; they are **soulish, not having the Spirit**. In Greek the word rendered *cause divisions* is *apodiorizo*. It is a rare word and has the sense of setting apart for the sake of classifying. The thought here is that these men **cause divisions** by separating people into groups, by claiming that their followers are more spiritual than the others. A common gnostic teaching is that all men can be divided into three categories: the fleshly (Gr. *sarkikoi*), the soulish, or those bound by the realm of the senses of this life (Gr. *psuchikoi*), and the truly spiritual (Gr. *pneumatikoi*). Naturally, they feel that *they* are the *pneumatikoi*, and those Christians who do not join them are the *psuchikoi*, the soulish ones, distinctly second-class.

Jude strips away this mask and reveals the truth. These men are not establishing a group of the spiritually elite. They are simply those who **cause divisions** and disturb the Church's unity. *They* are the **soulish** ones, men who are worldly, dominated by life in this world. Far from being spiritual, they do **not** even **have the Spirit**.

❧ EXCURSUS:
ON JUDE'S USE OF NON-CANONICAL BOOKS

Jude uses both the *Assumption of Moses* (alluding to the story in v. 9) and the *Book of Enoch* (quoting Enoch 1:9 in vv. 14–15)—books the Church did not ultimately include in its Old Testament canon of Scripture. What does this mean?

Both of these books are part of the Jewish apocalyptic literature that was produced in the centuries immediately preceding the coming of Christ. They were immensely popular among the Jews, especially (we may surmise) in the desperate days leading up to the destruction of Jerusalem in AD 70.

The Assumption of Moses is no longer extant, though several Church Fathers refer to it. The Book of Enoch is extant. Though written over time in the two centuries before Christ, it purports to be the work of Enoch, who was born in the seventh generation from Adam. Seven is the sacred number, and since Enoch "walked with God" and since "God took him" into heaven, so that he should not see death (Gen. 5:24; Heb. 11:5), it was thought likely that he should be privy to the mysteries of God.

Some have asked whether Jude, since he quotes these stories and sources, accepted the historicity of the narratives and believed that Enoch actually wrote the Book of Enoch, as well as whether Jude regarded them as canonical.

Regarding Jude and the historicity of these works, there

---

is no reason to think that the distinction between historical fact and legendary embellishment was as keen for him (or for ancients generally) as it is for us. Thus Paul is content to refer to a Jewish Targum (or Old Testament translation) that names two false prophets who opposed Moses in Egypt as "Jannes and Jambres" (2 Tim. 3:8–9), even though the names are not given in the canonical Old Testament, but are supplied by later Jewish legends. Paul uses these legends to make his point, with little regard for the entire question of the historicity of every detail.

This is not unlike Paul's use of pagan works and "prophecies," such as his citation of the pagan poet Aratus (quoted in Acts 17:28) or Epimenides (quoted in Titus 1:12). In the same way, the Jewish apocalyptic works were valued because they contained spiritual truth about God's Kingdom. The issue of strict historical accuracy did not arise for the ancients with the same importance as it does for us.

Thus Jude quotes the story of Michael and the devil from the Assumption of Moses in order to make a point about the humility of the angels—a humility that exists, even if the story quoted is ultimately deemed not historical. Similarly, Jude quotes from the Book of Enoch, putting the words in Enoch's mouth. The prophecy is true, whether or not Enoch actually uttered it. Jude writes to convey truth, not to sort out the minutiae of historical questions. As he contended for the souls of men in a life-and-death struggle against heresy, he used the weapons that were at hand, including the true lessons contained in the apocalyptic literary legacy of his people.

The question regarding the significance of Jude's citation of the work for the New Testament canon is more complicated. Certainly Jude quotes it as if it were Scripture, yet the Church did not ultimately include it in the canon. What does this mean?

The issue of the canon of Scripture is one that is too big

to deal with in detail here (indeed, one recent work dealing with this issue, *The Biblical Canon*, by L. M. McDonald, runs to over 500 pages). But I would suggest that the concept of a *closed* Old Testament canon—that is, an authoritative list which both includes some works and excludes all others—was absent from the mind of the first-century Church, so that it is anachronistic to assert that the Book of Enoch was (or was not) in Jude's Old Testament canon. Rather, I suggest, the whole question of canon did not exist for him as it does for us.

§III.   Final Admonitions (20–23)

ॐ ॐ ॐ ॐ ॐ

20 But you, beloved, building yourselves up on your most-holy faith, praying in the Holy Spirit;

21 keep yourselves in the love of God, anticipating the mercy of our Lord Jesus Christ for eternal life.

Jude then turns to positive exhortations. They must **keep** themselves **in the love of God**. Through their faith, they remain safe in God's love (compare v. 1), and if they make a stand against the heretics (the verb *keep* is in the aorist, indicating an accomplished action), they will keep themselves there. This involves three things: **building** themselves **up on** their **most-holy faith, praying in the Holy Spirit**, and **anticipating the mercy of our Lord Jesus Christ for eternal life**. (All these last three verbs are present participles in the Greek, whereas the verb *keep* is an aorist imperative; grammatically speaking, they are to **keep** themselves *by* **building, praying,** and **anticipating**.)

First of all, they are to **build** themselves **up on** their **most-holy faith**. The deposit of the faith is the foundation upon which their life in Christ is to be built; it is the unshakable rock on which the whole structure is to rest. They must cling to what the apostles have taught them.

Secondly, they are to **pray in the Holy Spirit**. The reference here is not just to fervent prayer (see Rom. 8:26; Eph. 6:18), but to prayer offered within the safety of the apostolic Church. The prayers of those who have fallen into immorality and heresy are not offered **in the Holy Spirit**, but from the unholy spirit of pride and delusion.

Thirdly, they are to **anticipate the mercy of our Lord Jesus Christ for eternal life**. The false teachers tend to deny that Christ is coming (see 2 Peter 3:3–4), but the faithful must live in expectation of His Return, walking in holiness (see 2 Peter 3:11). For when He comes, He will not bring them wrath, but **eternal life**.

ﾒﾟ ﾒﾟ ﾒﾟ ﾒﾟ ﾒﾟ

22 And have mercy on some who are disputing;
23 save others, snatching them from the fire; and
    on some have mercy with fear, hating even the
    garment stained by the flesh.

Brief exhortations follow about how to deal with those who are succumbing to heresy. (The textual tradition is not unanimous here; we follow that which lists three categories of people. Jude has a fondness for threes; compare "mercy, peace, and love" in v. 2, "Cain, Balaam, and Korah" in v. 11, "building, praying and anticipating" in vv. 20–21.)

Some in the church are **disputing**. The Greek is *diakrino* (used in v. 9), but it could also be rendered "doubting." It seems to describe those who are on the edge of falling into error, who are still arguing with themselves (and others), trying to decide whether or not to join the false teachers. The faithful must **have mercy** on them. They must not give them up for lost, but keep trying to lovingly draw them back to safety.

Others are already ensnared, like branches already piled on a blazing pyre. These they must save from the peril threatening to consume them, snatching them from the fire (compare the image in Zech. 3:2) before it is too late.

Some have been with the false teachers and now have come to see their error. On these they must have mercy with fear, accepting them back into the church, but taking care not to accept back any of their errors. Just as one **hates** a leprous **garment** and takes care not to touch it (Lev. 13:47f), so the faithful must reject the way of error, **stained** as it is **by the flesh** and sins of the world. Their love for the returning brother must not involve a lessening of revulsion for his former sins.

§IV.   Concluding Doxology (24–25)

> ❧ ❧ ❧ ❧ ❧
>
> 24 Now to Him who is able to guard you from tripping, and to stand you before His glory blameless, in exultation,
> 25 to the only God our Savior, through Jesus Christ our Lord, *be* glory, greatness, strength, and authority, before all the ages and now, and for all the ages. Amen.

Jude finishes his epistle with a cry of praise. Despite the care they must take not to trip and fall into heresy, the praise for their perseverance belongs not to them but to God. He is the One **who is able to guard** them **from tripping**. He is the source of all their wisdom; He is their strength. Through His care they can come safely home and **stand before His glory blameless, in exultation**.

They are called to **stand** upright, vindicated before His final judgment seat. They will be **blameless** (Gr. *amomos*) and will rejoice **in exultation** at their final salvation. This blamelessness refers to the quality of their life in this age. Those in the world (like the false teachers) walk in darkness and immorality, but the Christians are to be different. (Compare Phil. 2:15; Rev. 14:5.) This does not mean that Christians must be absolutely sinless, but it does mean that they are to have done with the sinful lifestyles of the world. A sacrifice that is "blameless" is acceptable to God (Ex. 29:1), and through our lives of penitent holiness, we offer ourselves as acceptable sacrifices to Him.

Finally, God is praised among the Gentiles as **the only God our Savior** (Jude's Jewish monotheism comes to the fore here), and he ascribes **glory, greatness, strength, and authority** to Him, from eternity past to eternity future. All of this is **through Jesus Christ our Lord**. He is the focus of the faith, the One through whom we come to the Father, and our praise of the Father is through Him.

Jude ends with **Amen**, expecting that his epistle (with its liturgical doxology) will be read in church, and that the faithful will respond to the doxology—and to all that he has said.

❧ The First Epistle of St. John ❧

Introduction

In his work on St. Francis, G. K. Chesterton spoke of "the stunning shrewdness which the unworldly can sometimes wield like a club of stone." That is, great saints can sometimes speak truth with such overwhelming simplicity that it startles and shakes us. St. John does this over and over again, in this epistle: "Everyone hating his brother is a murderer" (3:15); "the one not loving does not know God, because God is love" (4:8). The Beloved Disciple writes compellingly of love, and the starkness of the truth hits us like a club of stone. It provides a much-needed blow, for it can knock the lethal self-delusions out of our heads.

The work known as the First Epistle of John presents a bit of a puzzle, for unlike the Second and Third Epistles of John, the first epistle doesn't look much like an epistle, and nowhere claims to be written by John.

Nonetheless, the Church has never really doubted that it was written by John, the Beloved Disciple and apostle of the Lord. Its style greatly resembles that of the Gospel of John, and both the epistle and the Gospel claim to be written by eyewitnesses of Christ (John 21:24; 1 John 1:1–3). Also, the first epistle was obviously written by the same author as the second and third epistles, which explicitly bear the name of John. When Tertullian (born ca. 160) cites the epistle as being by "the apostle John" (*Against Marcion*, 5, 16), he is expressing the general view.

Though called an epistle, it has none of the marks of an epistle—no opening greetings, no opening prayer, no closing greetings. It seems to have been a tract, written for generalized distribution as a circular.

Why was it written and sent out? John was resident at Ephesus, and it was from here that he exercised his pastoral apostolic authority over the churches in the surrounding area, such as the churches in Asia (we note that Ephesus is the first church of the seven churches of Asia to which John's Apocalypse was sent; Rev. 2:1f). A heretical movement came to menace the churches in the area, and John wrote this tract to counteract its effects. It was sent out probably to those churches in Asia.

What was the nature of this heresy? It appears that the heretics had already withdrawn into groups of their own and formed their own schism (2:19). It also seems that there was a libertine streak to it and that they denied the reality of sin, saying that no matter how they lived, they had no guilt (1:8; 2:4; 3:6). They further appear to have asserted that Jesus was not the Christ, and that Christ had not come in the flesh (2:22; 4:2–3). Also, it seems they denied the saving power of the blood of Jesus on the Cross (1:7; 5:6).

A heretic, Cerinthus, about this time asserted that Jesus was not the Christ, but that the Christ-spirit came on Jesus at His baptism and left Him before His Cross. That is, the Christ-spirit did not actually become flesh, but simply rested on the human Jesus for a time. This also meant that Jesus' suffering on the Cross had no saving value (St. Irenaeus, *Against Heresies*, 1, 26, 1). John was known to have opposed Cerinthus's teaching and even fled from the public baths when Cerinthus entered (St. Irenaeus, *Against Heresies*, 3, 3). It is possible that the heresy opposed by John in this epistle was that of Cerinthus, or at least a type similar to his.

Whatever the exact nature of the heresy opposed in this epistle, it was an increasing threat. Their preachers were propagating it aggressively and throwing John's communities into doubt about the true nature of the faith. John writes to counteract the heresy and reestablish his flock in the fundamentals once delivered to them. He writes so that his flock can differentiate truth from error. The heretics claimed they were just presenting deeper truths. John writes so that the faithful can identify who the true Christians are.

It is difficult to fix a precise date to this epistle. It seems that John wrote his Gospel in the generation after the Synoptic Gospels of Matthew, Mark, and Luke, for the Fourth Gospel seems to pre-suppose familiarity with events mentioned in these other Gospels (thus John 11:2 mentions Mary's anointing of Jesus as a familiar event before narrating that anointing in 12:1f). If that Gospel was written late (perhaps about AD 85, from Ephesus), these epistles of John may well have been written about the same time.

❧ The First Epistle of St. John ❧

§I. Preface (1:1–4)

❧ ❧ ❧ ❧ ❧

1 1   What was from the beginning, what we have
heard, what we have seen with our eyes, what
we beheld and our hands touched, *this we
declare* about the word of life

2   (indeed the life was manifested, and we have
seen and witness and declare to you the eternal
life, which was with the Father and was manifested to us),

3   what we have seen and heard we declare also to
you, that you *yourselves* also may have sharing
with us. Indeed, our sharing *is* with the Father,
and with His Son Jesus Christ.

4   And these *things* we *ourselves* write, that our
joy may be fulfilled.

St. John begins his epistle with such a burst of enthusiasm that
his Greek is somewhat challenging. As an eyewitness, he proclaims
what he and the other apostles **have heard**, **what** they **have seen
with** their own **eyes**, **what** they **beheld and** their **hands touched**
(compare John 20:27; Luke 24:39)—namely Jesus Christ, He who
was from the beginning. (By opening with these words, *from the
beginning*, John evokes echoes of Genesis 1:1, which opens with like
words, and calls attention to the eternity and deity of Christ.) Jesus
is the subject of their proclamation **about the word** or message **of
life**, because it was in Jesus that **the life** of God **was manifested** on

the earth. The apostles **have seen** it for themselves and now **witness and declare** to all men **the eternal life** which is in the Son. It **was** eternally **with the Father and** in Jesus of Nazareth **was manifested** in time.

They do this that the readers of the epistle **also may have sharing with** them. The word rendered *sharing* is the Greek *koinonia*, sometimes rendered "fellowship," "communion." That is, the apostles **declare** what they have **seen and heard** in Christ that men everywhere may also come to experience what they have experienced, and thus join them in one unbroken fellowship of life. What they share together is indeed the eternal life made available in Christ, for their **sharing** [Gr. *koinonia*] *is* **with the Father, and with His Son Jesus Christ**. The apostles have come to share the life of the Father and the Son (compare John 5:25–26), and through their preaching, others come to share this also. It is by the acceptance of John's message (which includes their rejection of the heresy he warns them of) that his hearers can continue in this fellowship.

And these *things* we write (John uses the plural, for he writes as one of the apostles), that their **joy may be fulfilled**. (John probably wrote **our joy**, not "your joy," as some manuscripts have it.) In writing the epistle and thereby solidifying their connection with the apostolic fellowship, John finds his own joy completed. As a true pastor, he would grieve if any of his flock were lost (compare John 6:39; 17:12), and finds his joy fulfilled only if those he loves avoid the snares of heresy and deception.

§II.   Exhortation to Walk in Righteousness and Love, Separate from the World (1:5—5:12)

St. John now begins his letter proper, in which no progression of argument or ordered outline is readily discernible. Rather, he strings together a series of related exhortations, all aimed at warning his readers of the various errors menacing them in the form of the spreading heresy. Those who have gone into schism deny a number of fundamental truths. John writes to reaffirm these truths, telling his hearers that they must walk in righteousness and not be worldly and immoral as the schismatics are. They must confess Jesus as the true Christ, come in the flesh, dying on the Cross and shedding His Blood as the propitiation for their sins. They must love their brethren and not be filled with hate and pride, as are the schismatics. They must remain in the apostolic Church, clinging to the original message, for that is where the Spirit is to be found, and prayers are to be answered and forgiveness experienced.

Walking in the Light

5 And this is the news we have heard from Him and announce to you, that God is light, and in Him there is not any darkness.

6 If we say that we have sharing with Him and walk in the darkness, we lie and do not do the truth,

7 but if we walk in the light as He Himself is in the light, we have sharing with one another, and the blood of Jesus His Son cleanses us from every sin.

8 If we say that we do not have sin, we are deceiving ourselves, and the truth is not in us.

9 If we confess our sins, He is faithful and righteous that He may forgive us the sins and cleanse us from every unrighteousness.

10 If we say that we have not sinned, we make Him a liar, and His word is not in us.

2 1 My *little* children, I am writing these *things* to you that you may not sin. And if anyone sins, we have an Advocate with the Father, Jesus Christ *the* Righteous,

2 and He Himself is the propitiation for our sins, and not for ours only, but also for those of the whole world.

John begins by exhorting his hearers to righteousness. Having spoken of his firsthand witness of Christ, the apostle passes on **the news** he **has heard from Him**, the gist of Christ's teaching—**that God is light, and in Him there is not any darkness**. By saying that **God is light**, John speaks as a Jew. He is not expounding on the abstract nature of God (a very un-Jewish concern), but proclaiming God's character. God is altogether holy, altogether righteous. In **Him there is not any darkness**, no connivance at or acceptance of sin.

That means that **if we say that we have sharing** and fellowship **with Him**, and yet **walk in the darkness** of sin (as the heretics do), **we lie and do not do the truth**. The heretics' claim to know God more intimately is not credible, for their libertine lives of moral darkness prove they are far from Him who is Light. To **do the truth** means to live in faithfulness, with deeds wrought in God (compare John 3:21). Fellowship with and experience of God is only possible for those who live faithfully as He commanded.

If we do **walk in the light as He Himself is in the light**, being holy as He is holy, then **we have sharing with one another**. This **sharing** or fellowship (Gr. *koinonia*) refers to the experience of mutual fellowship in the apostolic Church. Open sin and rebellion will exclude one from sacramental fellowship in the Church, but righteous living allows one to keep one's place there. In that Church, **the blood of Jesus cleanses us from every sin**. For in the Church's eucharistic worship, the faithful receive cleansing of their sins.

If the faithful **confess** their **sins** (as the early Church did, as each confessed privately to God in preparation for coming to Sunday worship), then God will prove Himself **faithful and righteous**. He promised in Christ to forgive the sins of His people if they confessed them to Him, and He will do so, and **cleanse** them **from every unrighteousness** during their eucharistic service. The heretics are excluded from this fellowship—and therefore from this eucharistic cleansing.

These heretics, of course, deny their need for any such cleansing, for they claim not to incur guilt for anything they have done. They insist that they **do not have sin** or guilt and that their lives are acceptable to God as they are, despite their immoral lifestyles. For

John this just proves that they are **deceiving** themselves and that **the truth** is **not in** them. Their claim that they **have not sinned** in effect **makes** God **a liar**, for He promised forgiveness of sins through Christ, and here they are asserting that they have no sins to forgive. But God is not a liar. Rather, **His word is not in** them, and they have not experienced Him at all.

This assurance of sins' forgiveness does not mean, John hastens to add, that Christians may sin freely. St. John addresses them affectionately as **my *little* children** (Gr. *teknia*, a diminutive of *teknon*, "child"), and says that he is **writing these *things* that** they **may not sin**. Nonetheless, **if anyone sins**, the Church **has an Advocate with the Father, Jesus Christ *the* Righteous, and He Himself is the propitiation for our sins**, and not for those of the Church only, **but also for those of the whole world**. Christ is the Lamb of God who takes away the sin of the world (John 1:29) and calls the whole world into communion with Himself. The blood of the Cross washes clean the entire cosmos (Col. 1:20)—how much more is it effective to wash the sins of one sinner!

Jesus Christ is called *the* **Righteous**. This is not only a messianic title (see Acts 3:14; 7:52; 22:14); it also stresses that Christ, being righteous, is able to offer Himself as the unblemished and effective sacrifice for sins.

He is also called our **Advocate with the Father**. The title *advocate* is the Greek *paracletos*, used by Jesus in John 14:16 to refer to the Holy Spirit. The Greek is hard to translate; it literally means "someone called alongside" as a helper. In this context it has a legal feel to it, so that Christ comes to our aid as an intercessor before God's eternal justice. He ever lives as **the propitiation for our sins**, the means by which we are reconciled to the Father, the Mediator between God and men.

❧ EXCURSUS:
ON CHRIST AS THE PROPITIATION OF OUR SINS

Jesus Christ is called "the propitiation of our sins." The word translated here *propitiation* is the Greek *ilasmos*, used in the New Testament only here and in 4:10. There is some controversy about the meaning of this word and its proper translation in English.

Many prefer to translate it "expiation." What is the difference between the two terms? A person (in this case, God) is propitiated; sins are expiated. Some suggest that the idea of propitiating God suggests an unworthy idea of God—an angry, cantankerous Deity, one who needs to be mollified and calmed down by sacrifice. Indeed, the usual Latin word for the term is *placare*, from which the English word "placate" comes, and in the usual Greek literature of this time, the idea was indeed of propitiating and placating angry gods. Those who insist on the translation "expiation" contrast the (allegedly) unworthy concept of propitiating God with the (ostensibly) more Orthodox idea of expiating our sins. According to these translators, to say that God is a God of love means that He is not angry and needs no placating. The problem is not with God, they say; it is with our sins. Our sins need to be expiated and wiped out, but God needs no propitiating.

Admittedly, one needs to eliminate the pagan idea of the Father of our Lord Jesus being cantankerous and needing to be mollified, as if the Son were somehow at cross-purposes with the Father (no pun intended), and needed to calm Him down. The Son does not save us from the Father. Indeed, as John insists, the Father sent the Son as the Savior of the world (4:14).

Nonetheless, the concept of propitiation is not, in itself, unworthy, and does not in itself suggest the idea of appeasing bloodthirsty vengeance. But it does, however, suggest the reconciliation of two estranged parties, for our sins have estranged us from the Father. It is in this sense that Christ is the Mediator between God and men (1 Tim. 2:5).

The word *ilasmos* almost always means "propitiation," not "expiation," in secular Greek literature, and it would have meant this to John's readers. Further, the related verb *ilaskomai*, when used in the Greek Old Testament, often has the meaning of "propitiate" (e.g. 2 Kg. 24:4; Lam. 3:42; Dan. 9:19). The related word *exilaskomai* is used in the Greek Septuagint Old Testament to translate the Hebrew word *kapar*, "to cover, to make atonement, to divert the divine anger."

The Hebrew concept of sacrifice is indeed one of propitiation—compare, for example, the sacrifice of Noah in Genesis 8:20–21, with its "soothing aroma," or the incense sacrifice of Aaron in Numbers 16:45–48, when the sacrifice averted God's wrath in a plague of judgment. The sacrifices of the Law were for propitiating God. Certainly this needs to be interpreted in a way that is worthy of God. Any idea that God is actually calmed down should be seen as literary anthropomorphism, the use of human images and activities to describe God (compare talk of "God's arm" in Ps. 98:1). But the concept must not be emptied of all meaning. The truth is that our sins have provoked the justice of God *precisely because He is good*, and sacrifice is offered to reconcile us to Him. Our sins have estranged us from God and made us fit objects of the divine wrath (see Eph. 5:6). Because of His great love for us, the Father has provided the Son as the propitiation for our sins, that we might be reconciled to Him.

ॐ ॐ ॐ ॐ ॐ

3 And by this we know that we have come to know Him, if we keep His commandments.

4 The one saying, "I have come to know Him," and not keeping His commandments is a liar, and the truth is not in this one.

5 But whoever keeps His word, in this one the love of God has truly been perfected. By this we know that we are in Him:

> 6   the one who says he remains in Him **ought himself to walk thus as He walked.**

The heretics, even though they live immoral lives, claim to have a special and deeper knowledge of God than the rank-and-file Christians. St. John says that it is **by this** that all may **know** whether or not they have truly **come to know Him**, **if** they **keep His commandments**, for the one claiming such knowledge and **not keeping His commandments is a liar.** Such a person does not know God. Whatever his claims of knowing deeper truths, **the truth is not in this one** at all, and he has never experienced God. The one who truly knows God **keeps His word** and lives as Jesus commanded—**in this one the love of God has truly been perfected.** That is, God's love for him has truly taken root in his heart, bearing fruit in love for others. Thus it is **by this** that **we know that we are in Him** and are truly doing His will: **the one who says he remains in** Christ **ought himself to walk thus as He walked.** The heretics claim to follow Christ's will more perfectly than others, but they do not walk and live as Jesus did. That proves that their claim to remain in Christ and be His disciples is a false claim.

> ৵ঌ   ৵ঌ   ৵ঌ   ৵ঌ   ৵ঌ
>
> 7   Beloved, I am not writing to you a new commandment, but an old commandment which you have had from the beginning; the old commandment is the word which you heard.
>
> 8   Again, I am writing to you a new commandment, which is true in Him and in you, because the darkness is passing away, and the true light is already shining.
>
> 9   The one saying he is in the light and hating his brother is in the darkness until now.
>
> 10   The one loving his brother remains in the light, and there is not a stumbling-block in him.
>
> 11   But the one hating his brother is in the

> darkness and walks in the darkness, and does
> not know where he goes because the darkness
> has blinded his eyes.

The apostle stresses that he is **not writing** to them **a new commandment, but an old commandment which** they **have had from the beginning** of their Christian experience. This is no innovation, but a return to the fundamentals they have always known as reliable. His teaching has proven itself over time.

Again, and on the other hand, he acknowledges there *is* a sense in which he is **writing** to them **a new commandment**, for Christ's commandment is characteristic of the new Kingdom that He brings. This commandment is embodied in Jesus' love for His own (John 13:34), and this love is something that this old age has never seen before. The truth of this commandment, and how it belongs not to this age but to the new age to come, is realized in the life of Jesus and in the lives of His disciples—it is **true in Him and in** them. For both Jesus and His disciples shine with a love never before experienced, and men look at the Church and exclaim, "Behold how these Christians love one another!" His disciples belong no longer to this world, but to the world to come, and **the darkness** of this world is already **passing away**. In the Church, **the true light** of the age to come **is already shining** for all to see. In the Church, the Kingdom to come is already here.

The heretics may claim to be in the light. But they are obviously **in the darkness until now**, helpless to find their way to the light. How can one tell? Because **the one loving his brother** is the one who **remains in the light**, and in such a one **there is not a stumbling-block**. The one who loves will not stumble or fall into the guilt that apostates will incur. (To stumble is to fall into apostasy; compare John 16:1.) But the heretics do not love the brothers, but hate them, and **the one hating his brother is in the darkness**. They claim superior spiritual illumination, but have none. Such a one **does not know where he goes because the darkness has blinded his eyes**. Whatever his vaunted claims, he is utterly incapable of guiding anyone.

Believers and the World

> ❧ ❧ ❧ ❧ ❧
>
> 12 I am writing to you, *little* children, because your sins are forgiven you for His Name's sake.
> 13 I am writing to you, fathers, because you have known Him who has been from the beginning.
> I am writing to you, young men, because you have conquered the Evil One.
> 14 I have written to you, children, because you have known the Father.
> I have written to you, fathers, because you have known Him who has been from the beginning.
> I have written to you, young men, because you are strong, and the Word of God remains in you, and you have conquered the Evil One.

St. John then writes a pair of triads, outlining in broad strokes the main points of the message he is writing to them. He writes to them **because** of certain truths, to remind his hearers of them and reestablish their hearts in them. To this end he repeats himself, first saying, **I am writing**, and then saying **I have written** in order to stress his message.

He first writes in verse 12 to all his hearers, addressing them as *little* **children** (Gr. *teknia*), as he does in 2:1, 28; 3:7, 18; 5:21. His message to all is that their **sins are forgiven** them **for His Name's sake**. The heretics deny the reality of sin and the need for forgiveness, but John will have all remember that sin is indeed a reality, and that in the Church their sins have been forgiven because of their relationship to Jesus, since they call upon His Name. (Compare 3 John 7: to go out "for the sake of the *Name*" is to go out for the sake of *Jesus*.)

He repeats an admonition to all his hearers, his **children** (Gr. *paidia*; compare 3:18), in verse 14a, this time reminding them that they **have known the Father** and truly experienced God, unlike the heretics, who have not known God (2:4). This knowledge of the Father also has to do with Jesus, for it is through Jesus that we have access to the Father and know the Father (John 14:6; Eph. 2:18). The one who has the Son thereby has the Father as well, for the Son and the Father are one (John 10:30; 1 John 2:23).

After the general exhortations to all the children of God, John turns to two groups within them, the older believers and the younger ones. (Compare exhortations to groups of older and younger men in 1 Peter 5:5 and 1 Tim. 5:1.) The older believers, those who have been in Christ for some time, John calls **fathers** (Gr. *pater*); the younger ones he calls **young men** (*neaniskos*).

John addresses the **fathers** first. He reminds them in verse 13a that they have **known Him who has been from the beginning**, namely, Jesus Christ (compare 1:1). That is, they have known the eternal Word, and will not be misled by heretical distortions that say Jesus is not the Christ (2:22) or that He has not come in the flesh (4:2–3). John repeats this reminder to the fathers in verse 14b, using exactly the same words, urging them again to cling to the truth about Christ which they have long held.

John also addresses the **young men**, reminding them in verse 13b that they **have conquered the Evil One**. This reminder is expanded in verse 14c with the additional comments that they **are strong** and the **Word of God remains in** them. That is why they are able to conquer the Evil One—because the Word of God, the apostolic teaching about Jesus, has made them strong. Despite the relative inexperience of these younger believers, they have still prevailed against the foe—and must continue to do so!

This victory over the Evil One is not just a matter of overcoming daily temptations to sin. Something more cosmic is meant. For John, the Evil One is not just a tempter of individuals. Rather, the whole world lies in his power (5:19). Our faith, however, gives us conquest and victory (Gr. *nike*) over the world (5:4). By **conquering**

[Gr. *nikao*] **the Evil One**, John therefore means that we have over-come the lies and propaganda which have ensnared the world, and remain free in the truth. Despite the lies of the heretics, the young believers have not fallen prey to them, but have conquered.

> ॐ   ॐ   ॐ   ॐ   ॐ
>
> 15 Do not love the world, nor the things in the world. If anyone loves the world, the love of the Father is not in him,
> 16 because all that *is* in the world, the desire of the flesh, and the desire of the eyes, and the pretension of life's *possessions*, is not from the Father, but is from the world.
> 17 And the world is passing away, and its desire, but the one doing the will of God remains forever.

Building on these reminders of verses 12–14, St. John urges his hearers **not** to **love the world, nor the things in the world**. This is the way of the heretics, who in their lifestyles and philosophical approaches are utterly worldly (4:5). But as those who have **the love of the Father in** them, the Christians must be different, for they cannot love both the Father and the world.

This is because **all that *is* in the world is not from the Father, but is from the world**. Here "the world" stands in stark contrast to "the Father." By *the world*, John here means not God's creation (as in John 3:16), but the great idol, the world as proudly self-contained and self-sufficient, the world as rival to God. Both the Father and the world claim the heart's total allegiance, and one must choose whom to serve. The Father is characterized by light and love (1:5; 4:8). The world, however, is characterized by all the things in it: **the desire of the flesh, and the desire of the eyes, and the pretension of life's *possessions***. That is, the world is characterized by sensuality and lust (**the desire of the flesh**); by the greedy craving to acquire all that one can see (**the desire of the eyes**); and by the braggart's pride that competes vainly with others over possessions and delights to crow over rivals (**the pretension of life's *possessions***). Obviously such things are not from the Father, and one cannot love these things and love the Father too.

In fact, **the world is passing away, and its desire** as well. One should not give one's heart to something so ephemeral as the world. It is not just doomed to pass away one day—its final dissolution has already begun (the verb rendered *pass away*—Gr. *paragetai*—is in the present tense). That is, God has already given the world its death sentence, and it is on the way out. The Kingdom of God established in its midst is a token and promise that its end is near. The world's **desire** and lust (its animating heart) will perish with it—taking along those whose love and desire is for the world. It is only **the one doing the will of God**, the one loving the Father and not the world, who will **remain forever**. Such a one will never pass away when the world does, but will abide and reign to ages of ages, outshining and outlasting the sun and the stars.

Antichrists

> ৯৮ ৯৮ ৯৮ ৯৮ ৯৮
>
> 18 Children, it is the last hour; and as you heard that an antichrist is coming, even now many antichrists have come; from which we know that it is the last hour.
> 19 They went out from us, but they were not from us, for if they had been from us, they would have remained with us, but *they went out*, that it might be manifested that they all are not from us.
> 20 But you *yourselves* have an anointing from the Holy One, and you all know.

John addresses his hearers as beloved **children** (Gr. *paidia*) and warns them again of the heretics spreading their confusion and their false claims. The faithful should not be shaken by such things—after all, **it is the last hour**. They have heard from all the apostles that in the last days **an antichrist is coming**. This has proven true, for **even now many antichrists have come**, and that proves that it is indeed **the last hour**. By "the last hour," John is not measuring time according to the calendar, but according to God's eschatological purposes. He does not mean that the Second Coming is but a few years away, but that it is the next thing on the divine agenda. In Christ, history reached its goal and culmination. All that remains now is for Him to return and judge the world. The time immediately preceding this return (that is, the time between the Ascension of Christ and His Second Coming) is what St. John means by "the last hour."

This time of the last hour is to be characterized by increasing polarity between light and darkness, between the power of God and the opposing power of Satan. All of the apostles referred to this escalated conflict characteristic of these eschatological days. Paul wrote that dangerous times would come (2 Tim. 3:1), and that eventually the conflict would come to a head in a final persecution of the Church led by the "man of lawlessness" (2 Thess. 2:3f).

Most of the apostolic warnings about these times of conflict, however, have to do with false teachers, threats from *within* the Church. Thus Paul warns of "savage wolves" arising from within the Church who will "draw disciples after them" (Acts 20:29–30). He speaks of Christians "leaving the faith, paying attention to teachings of demons" (1 Tim. 4:1f). Peter warns that in the last days, "mockers will come," "false-teachers who will sneak in destructive factions" and heresies (2 Peter 3:3; 2:1). Jude reminds his hearers of "the words spoken before by the apostles," warning of mockers appearing "in the last time" (Jude 17–18). Apparently, apostolic warnings of heretical schisms to come were commonplace.

I would suggest that this is what John means by reminding his hearers that they have **heard that an antichrist is coming**. The term "antichrist" later became a title for the final adversary to appear just before the Second Coming, the one outside the Church (called by Paul "the man of lawlessness"; 2 Thess. 2:4) who will launch the final great persecution. It is easy to read this meaning back into John's use of the term, even though that final persecutor is never called by the Scriptures "the Antichrist." What St. John means here by saying that all have **heard that an antichrist is coming** is that they have heard of the rise of heretical teaching, Satan's counterfeit and opposition to the work of Christ (compare 4:3). This is "the antichrist" of which they have been warned (2:22). John's point here is not, "The final Antichrist will come eventually, but even now there are many little antichrists as his forerunners." His point is rather, "You have heard that an antichrist is coming—that prediction has been fulfilled, for even now there are *many* antichrists." St. John mentions the many antichrists *as the fulfillment of the prophecy* that antichrist would come.

The false teachers, therefore, are not simply another variant of Christianity. Rather, they are Satan's counterfeit, long expected. Though **they went out from us**, breaking away from the Church in schism, they are not a legitimate offshoot. They have nothing in common with the Church of their ostensible origins and **were not** really **from us, for if they** really **had been from us, they would have remained with us,** and not gone into schism. The fact of schism proves them to be of an alien spirit. But, St. John adds, as for his hearers (the **you** is emphatic in the Greek), they **have an anointing from the Holy One** (from Christ, who gives the Spirit; compare John 6:69; 16:7), **and** they **all know**.

What is this **anointing** (Gr. *chrisma*)? It is the spiritual component of their chrismation, that part of their baptism when they were anointed with oil and received the laying on of hands for the reception of the Holy Spirit. (Tertullian, born about 160, describes this as part of baptism in his work *On Baptism*, ch. 7.) By the power of the Spirit given to each Christian, each of them can know spiritual truth when he encounters it, be he ever so humble. The Spirit is not the possession solely of the elite (as the false teachers claim themselves to be). All of the faithful have the Spirit and the ability to discern the truth, and need not be taken in by pretended gnostic revelations.

This anointing should not be taken to imply individual infallibility of judgment in all things, as if the individual were sufficient to himself and did not need to be taught. Rather, John simply means that a believer, taught by the apostolic tradition and indwelt by the Spirit, experiences the peace of God when he responds to the authentic Gospel (compare 5:10), and that by that Spirit he can detect a demonic counterfeit when he meets it.

> ❧ ❧ ❧ ❧ ❧
>
> 21 I have not written to you because you do not know the truth, but because you know it, and because no lie is from the truth.
> 22 Who is the liar, but the one denying that Jesus is the Christ? This one is the antichrist, the one denying the Father and the Son.
> 23 Everyone denying the Son does not have the Father either; the one confessing the Son has the Father also.

The gnostic schismatics claim a special gift of the Spirit that enables them to impart new truths. John insists that, though speaking of the anointing of the Spirit, he is not doing that. He has **not written** to them **because** they **do not know the truth**, as if to make up for some defect in the apostolic deposit of teaching they have received. There is no defect in that teaching. He writes **because** they *do* **know** the truth, and, since **no lie is from the truth**, he writes to warn them of that gnostic lie.

For **who is the liar**, indeed, the liar *par excellence*, and how can a lie be recognized? **The one denying that Jesus is the Christ**, this is the liar, **the antichrist** long expected, for such are **denying the Father** as well as **the Son**. The schismatics may protest that they are not denying the Father, but John is adamant. To deny the Son is thereby to deny the Father also, so that **everyone denying the Son does not have the Father either**. Their lies about the Son mean that they have forfeited all share in God, whereas **the one** truly **confessing the Son has the Father also**. The Father and the Son are one, and true faith in Jesus means that one possesses all of God.

In what sense, though, do these heretics deny that Jesus is the Christ? Probably not (as the unbelieving Jews of John's Gospel did) by simply denying that Jesus of Nazareth is the Messiah. John is dealing with people who were once (nominally) part of the Church (v. 19); he is dealing with Christological heresy, not simple unbelief. There are some in his day, like Cerinthus, who say that the divine Christ-spirit came on Jesus at His baptism, but left Him before the Cross. For these people, Jesus was not the Christ; He only was united to the Christ for a while. It would seem that this heresy (or one like it) is the Christological heresy dealt with here.

In our day of easy tolerance of almost any theological opinion, it is easy to blame John (and the apostolic Church) for being too hard on heretics. After all, anybody can make a mistake! But these heresies were not simple mistakes made by men who wanted to know the truth. They were deliberate attempts to subvert the teaching of the apostles to make it more palatable to the world—and all for selfish ends. A heresy is not an error, like a mistake in doing sums. It is a deliberate rejection of truth, an embrace of the darkness, a prideful choice of one's own ideas over received Tradition.

ॐ ॐ ॐ ॐ ॐ

24 *And* you, that which you heard from the beginning, let *that* remain in you. If what you heard from the beginning remains in you, you *yourselves* also will remain in the Son and in the Father.

25 And this is the promise which He *Himself* promised to us: eternal life.

26 These *things* I have written to you about those deceiving you.

27 And you, the anointing which you received from Him remains in you, and you have no need that anyone should teach you; but as His anointing teaches you about everything, and is true and is not a lie, and as it has taught you, remain in Him.

As for John's hearers (the **you** is emphatic), they will be safe from such lies if they **let remain** in them **that which** they **heard from the**

beginning. Clinging to the apostolic tradition they received when they were converted is a sufficient safeguard against losing the Father and the Son. If they cling to that, remaining unmoved by heretical temptations to discard it, they will **remain in the Son**, as part of His true Church, His Body—and thereby remain **in the Father** also. **And this is the promise which He *Himself*** (i.e. the Son; compare John 17:2) **promised to us: eternal life**. That is, the result of remaining in the Son and in the Father is that they are promised eternal life. John here stresses the future element of our eternal life (calling it **the promise which He promised**) because of the possibility of losing it. If we remain in Christ, we have that promise held out to us—let us not lose it through falling into heresy.

For his part, St. John says, he has **written these *things* about those deceiving** them, lest they succeed in their attempts. For his hearers' part (the **you** is again emphatic), they must not only heed John's message, but also rely on **the anointing which** they **received from Him,** which **remains in** them. The anointing of the Spirit they received from Christ when they were chrismated has not abandoned them. They can rely on this inner discernment to **teach** them **about everything** pertaining to salvation. It **is true and is not a lie** (like the pretended spiritual insights of the heretics). **As it has taught** them in the past, confirming for their hearts the truth of the apostolic Gospel, so they must heed its teaching now and **remain in Him**, not leaving the Lord to accept the heretical counterfeit. They have **no need that anyone** (such as the gnostics) **should teach** them further truths. The anointing of the Spirit confirms that the apostolic tradition is all they need.

Abiding in Hope

> ❧ ❧ ❧ ❧ ❧
>
> 28 And now, *little* children, remain in Him, that if He is manifested we may have boldness, and not be ashamed *and shrink* from Him at His Coming.
>
> 29 If you know that He is righteous, you know

> that everyone also doing the righteousness has
> been born from Him.

John therefore exhorts his hearers, as his *little* children (Gr. *teknia*), to **remain in** Jesus by resisting the lies of the heretics. That way, **if He is manifested** at His Second Coming in their day, they **may have boldness** to stand before Him unashamed and receive the promised eternal life. If they are to leave the truth for the lies of the schismatics, they will **be ashamed *and shrink* from Him at His Coming**, to be banished eternally from His presence with other lawless men.

For this is why the heretics will be rejected on the Last Day—not because their opinions are wrong, but because they are not righteous, because they refuse to repent of their sins. The children of God—those who will be saved on that Day—are righteous and love Jesus (see John 14:21). One can **know** who the true children of God are by looking at Jesus—**He is righteous**, and so **everyone also doing the righteousness has** obviously **been born from Him**. The righteous life of the believer reveals his family connection and his true sonship.

(It appears that the **He** that is **righteous** in verse 29 refers to Christ, the immediate antecedent. If this is so, St. John also seems to speak of believers who were **born from** Christ. This is perhaps a reference to their baptismal rebirth, in which they become children of God the Father *through* Christ, His Son. In this rebirth, the Son and the Father are so united that John here applies the usual language of being "born from God" to Christ.)

ॐ ॐ ॐ ॐ ॐ

3 1   See what sort of love the Father has given to us, that we should be called children of God; and we are. For this *reason* the world does not know us, because it did not know Him.

2   Beloved, now we are children of God, and it has not yet been manifested what we will be. We

> know that, when He is manifested, we will be
> like Him, because we will see Him as He is.
> 3 And everyone having this hope in Him purifies
> himself, just as that One is pure.

John then cries out, **See what sort of love the Father has given to us, that we should be called children of God**! That in baptism God should **call** and adopt us as His own children—we who have sinned and spurned His love times without number—how astonishing and undeserved is this **love**! (The verb rendered *call* is in the aorist tense, indicating a completed event, such as their earlier baptism.) And yet thus we are, in reality, beyond anything we could have dared hope.

The fact that we are God's children, however, is not recognized by the world. Instead, the world rejects our message and even persecutes us. It is **for this *reason***, of course, that **the world does not know us—it did not know Him**. It did not recognize Jesus as God's Son, and so naturally does not recognize His disciples as God's children either (see John 15:20).

Nonetheless, even **now we are children of God**, despite the blindness of the world to this fact. But **it has not yet been manifested what we will be** in the age to come. Now we are slandered and spurned; then we will be vindicated and honored. Now we are persecuted and killed; then we will be immortal and glorious. **When Christ is manifested** on the Last Day, **we will be like Him**, sharing His divine nature and glory, **because we will see Him as He is**. In this age we see comparatively dimly; but then we will see Him face to face (1 Cor. 13:12). It is because of His unveiled presence and power that we will be changed to be like Him (1 Cor. 15:49–53).

St. John presents this shining hope of eternal life as an incentive to persevere in righteousness. For **everyone having this hope in Him purifies himself, just as that One is pure**. They know that a righteous life is required of them if they would stand before Him boldly at His Judgment, and so they purify themselves, living lives of moral purity, just as Jesus Himself (an emphatic **that One**, Gr. *ekeinos*) is pure (compare 2:6). This does not, of course, mean that utter sinlessness is required. It does mean that the Christians must live differently than the world does, striving to live in love (3:14). In this they are different from the heretics, for they do not purify themselves of sin, but walk after the lusts of the flesh, of the eyes, and the pretensions of life's possessions (compare 2:16).

The Righteousness of God's Children

꒰꒱ ꒰꒱ ꒰꒱ ꒰꒱ ꒰꒱

4 Everyone doing the sin also does the lawlessness, and the sin is the lawlessness.

5 And you know that that One was manifested that He might take away sins; and in Him is not sin.

6 No one remaining in Him sins; no one sinning has seen Him or known Him.

7 *Little* children, let no one deceive you; the one doing the righteousness is righteous, even as that One is righteous;

8 the one doing the sin is from the devil, because the devil has sinned from the beginning. The Son of God was manifested for this *purpose*, that He might destroy the works of the devil.

9 No one who is born from God does sin, because His seed remains in him; and he is not able to sin, because he has been born from God.

10 By this the children of God and the children of the devil are manifest: anyone not doing righteousness is not from God, also the one not loving his brother.

11 For this is the news which you have heard from the beginning, that we love one another;

12 not as Cain, *who* was from the Evil One and slaughtered his brother. And for what cause did he slaughter him? Because his works were evil, and his brother's *were* righteous.

St. John encourages his hearers to live differently from these heretics by pointing out that **everyone doing the sin also** thereby **does the lawlessness, for sin is**, in essence, **lawlessness**. By *lawlessness* (Gr. *anomia*) John does not mean just a breaking of God's Law. The word is used in 2 Thess. 2:4 with respect to the final adversary of God, the "man of lawlessness," the embodiment of Satan's rebellion. "Lawlessness" here means the eschatological opposition to God characteristic of the last days. **Doing sin** might seem to be of little importance (it certainly is for the heretics), but John asserts that all sin is of extreme importance, for to sin means to align oneself against God, just as the devil does.

Further, John reminds them that **that One** (emphatic, Gr. *ekeinos*), Jesus, **was manifested that He might take away sins** on the Cross, purging away sin's guilt and nullifying its power. His opposition to sin is total, for **in Him is not sin**. He is completely righteous and is the enemy of all sin.

Thus, **no one remaining in Him sins**; in fact, **no one sinning has seen Him or known Him**. To be united to Jesus the Righteous One means that one is righteous, so that a life of sin proves that one is not united to Him and has never experienced Him.

John addresses them affectionately as *little* **children**, urging them not to let the heretics **deceive** them with their false claims. The heretics claim to be the truly righteous ones, the chosen ones who know the deep mysteries of God.

John cuts through such nonsense, saying that **the one doing the righteousness is** the one who is **righteous, even as that One**, Jesus, **is righteous**. One must imitate Jesus to lay true claim to be one of the righteous chosen ones. The heretics live lives of worldliness and sin, and so obviously have no claim to call themselves the **righteous** chosen ones of God. Rather, since they are **doing sin**, they are **from the devil. The devil has sinned from the beginning** of history, lying and seducing men into sin, and since these heretics live lives of sin, they belong to the devil. They do not belong to the Son of God, for **the Son of God was manifested for this** very *purpose,* **that He might destroy the works of the devil**, obliterating the sin that characterizes their lives. The heretics are not born from God as they claim, for **no one who is born from God does** (or "commits"; Gr. *poieo*) **sin**.

Such behavior is impossible for one born from God, **because His seed remains in him**, so that he **is not able to sin**. What is this **seed**? The metaphor is that of transmission of life, for human life was thought of as being transmitted through the imparting of seed. John therefore here speaks of the gift of the divine life within us, Christ dwelling in our hearts (Eph. 3:17), the Father and Son together making a home within us (John 14:23). In this divine presence within us, sin finds no place, and so those truly indwelt by God cannot do sin.

Thus, **by this** both the **children of God and the children of the devil are manifest** and may be recognized: **anyone not doing righteousness is not from God**, which includes **the one not loving his brother**. This necessity of love is not a new revelation. It is **the news which** they have **heard from the beginning** of their Christian walk, for they were commanded to **love one another** (John 13:34). If they refuse this and keep prideful hatred and disdain boiling in their hearts, they will be like **Cain**. He was not from God, but **from the Evil One**, for Cain **slaughtered his brother** Abel, just as the Evil One was a murderer from the beginning also (Gen. 4:1f; John 8:44). And **for what cause did** Cain **slaughter him? Because his works were evil, and his brother's** *were* **righteous**—that is, because Cain saw that Abel was fundamentally different from him. Cain's murder of Abel reveals the essential and timeless incompatibility of righteousness and sin, the stark difference between the children of God and those of the devil—and therefore between the faithful Christians and the heretics.

❧ EXCURSUS:
ON SIN AND THE CHRISTIAN

A word must be said about John's statement that "no one remaining in Him sins . . . the one doing sin is of the devil" (3:6, 8). It is obvious that John is not saying that Christians are incapable of committing a sin, or that those who commit a sin are of the devil. Indeed, John himself begins his epistle by acknowledging that Christians commit sin (1:10), and he warns against this in such a way as to show that it must be a real possibility (e.g. 2:1). What then does he mean by saying that the one doing sin is of the devil and is not a Christian at all?

It is important to recognize that John is not penning an abstract treatise on sin, but rather warning Christians of a specific threat—namely, the heretics who entice them with claims of deeper knowledge of God. The lives of these heretics were characterized by sin and lovelessness. John's words in this chapter are aimed at them, and he says that their untransformed lives prove their claims of knowing God are false. John therefore is not saying that Christians commit no sin; he is saying that sin does not characterize their lives (as it does the lives of the heretics).

It is helpful to look carefully at John's words. He sometimes uses the verb "to sin" (Gr. *amartano*), but also the phrase "doing the sin" (Gr. *poion ten amartian*; 3:4, 8, 9). This phrase is parallel to other phrases such as "doing the truth" (1:6), "doing the righteousness" (2:29; 3:7, 10), "doing the lawlessness" (3:4), "doing the things pleasing before Him" (3:22). In his Gospel, John also speaks of "doing the truth" (John 3:21), which seems to be paired with its opposite, "practicing base things" (John 3:20; Gr. *prasson phaula*). By using the word "doing" (Gr. *poieo*), John seems to have in mind something habitual, parallel with "practicing" (Gr. *prasso*; John 3:20). This confirms that what St. John means here is that Christians do not live lives of sin, as worldlings do, because this is contrary to their new nature in Christ and His presence abiding in them. It does not mean that they cannot sin on occasion. Throughout this chapter, John is contrasting the lifestyles of the Christian and the worldling.

ॐ ॐ ॐ ॐ ॐ

13 Do not marvel, brothers, if the world hates you.

14 We *ourselves* know that we have passed over from death into life, because we love the brothers. The one not loving remains in death.

15 Everyone hating his brother is a murderer; and you know that no murderer has eternal life remaining in him.

16 We have known love by this, because that One laid down His life for us, and we *ourselves* ought to lay down our lives for the brothers.

17 But whoever has the world's life-*possessions*, and observes his brother having a need and closes his heartfelt *love* against him, how *does* the love of God remain in him?

18 *Little* children, let us not love with word or with tongue, but in work and truth.

19 By this we will know that we are from the truth, and will persuade our heart before Him,

20 whenever our heart condemns *us*, for God is greater *than* our heart and knows all *things*.

21 Beloved, if our heart does not condemn us, we have boldness before God;

22 and whatever we ask we receive from Him, because we keep His commandments and do the things pleasing before Him.

23 And this is His commandment, that we believe in the Name of His Son Jesus Christ, and love one another, as He gave a commandment to us.

24 And the one keeping His commandments remains in Him, and He in him. And by this we know that He remains in us, by the Spirit whom He has given us.

Cain killed Abel because he saw in Abel someone fundamentally different from himself, and this is also why **the world hates the Christians**. Those in the world, being spiritually xenophobic, also recognize that the Christians are alien to themselves, and they persecute them for this reason. John's hearers must **not marvel** at this (which they might, if they thought themselves part of the world), but remember that they are part of the world no longer. The evidence that they no longer belong to the world but **have passed over from death into life** is that they do not hate their fellow Christians (which they would if they were of the world), but rather **love the brothers**.

Indeed, **the one not loving remains in death**, just as the world remains in death. How could the world not remain in death? For **everyone hating his brother** (as the world hates the Christians) **is a murderer** like Cain, and all **know that no murderer has eternal life remaining in him**. Hatred of a brother is the root and essence of murder (even as Cain hated Abel, which led to his murder), and a murderer deserves death. Thus it is obvious that a murderer (that is, one who lives in hate) will not be rewarded with eternal life.

And if hatred is known by *taking* life (as Cain took Abel's life), so **love** is **known by this**—by **that One** (Jesus) *giving* life, for He **laid down His life** for the Christians and for the whole world. If the Christians would love and not hate, they therefore **ought to lay down** their **lives for the brothers**. For this is what the love of the brothers (v. 14) means—to die for them, even as Christ died. What is involved in this dying? John gives an example: **whoever has the world's life-*possessions*, and observes his brother having a need**, he must give to him. If he does not, but **closes his heartfelt *love***, his inmost compassion (Gr. *splagxna*), **against him** and refuses to help him, **how *does* the love of God remain in him?** Obviously such a one does *not* love, but remains in death (see v. 14b). God's love has obviously not taken root in such a person (compare 2:5), and he has never experienced Him.

St. John addresses his hearers tenderly as *little* **children** (Gr. *teknia*) and urges them **not** to **love with word or with tongue** only, **but** also **in work and truth**. Loving in words alone reveals us as part of the world. Only by our loving in deed is it shown that we have passed from death into life. Claims to love the brothers are cheap enough to make, but such fine words need to be followed up by actions.

This love is the basis on which we can **know that we are from the truth,** and **persuade our heart** of it **whenever our heart condemns us**. Indeed, **God is greater** *than* **our heart and knows all** *things*—including the reality of our love. In this last clause, John has a play on words: our hearts may **condemn** us (Gr. *kataginosko*), but God **knows** all (Gr. *ginosko*). God's true knowledge of our lives is set against the false doubts sown in our hearts. In our prayers **before Him,** He will confirm our hearts in the truth, for His power is greater than any lie.

In speaking about our hearts condemning us, John is referring, not to the pangs of conscience, but to doubts sown by the heretics about the reality of the Christians' spiritual experience. With their vaunted false claims to deeper knowledge, the heretics have begun to persuade the Christians that perhaps they are right after all, and that the Christians should abandon their own ways to follow them instead. Whenever these doubts arise, the faithful may **persuade** their **heart** that they are **from the truth** and resist temptations to such apostasy. Remembering how love reigns among the Christians and is notably absent among the heretics should convince them where the truth lies and who is really of God.

If their **heart does not condemn** them, then they will remain in the true Church, unmoved by doubts sown by heretics, and **have boldness before God** in the Church's liturgical prayers. (The word rendered *boldness* is the Gr. *parresia*, indicating the freedom to speak anything, as to a friend.) Then **whatever** they **ask** they will **receive from Him**, according to Christ's promise to His Church, for those of the true Church **keep His commandments and do the things pleasing before Him** (John 14:14–15; 15:16). The context is ecclesial, not individual. John refers primarily to the authentic Church standing before God in assembled prayer, with authority to petition the Father through His Son.

The gist of these commandments—the things that please Him

187

and make us acceptable to Him—is that **we believe in the Name of His Son Jesus Christ, and love one another**, as Jesus Himself **gave a commandment to us** (see John 6:29; 13:34). Both orthodox belief and authentic love are what Christ requires—and these are absent from the communities of the heretics. **The one keeping** these **commandments**—observing faith and love—**remains in** God, and God remains **in him**. He should remember this, and not fear that he is wrong in not joining the heretics. And they can **know** that God **remains in** them by a further piece of evidence—**by the Spirit whom He has given** them.

Reference to **the Spirit** is also ecclesial, in that John refers to the works of the Spirit in the Church assemblies, such as healings, exorcisms, overflowing joy, and the prophetic gifts. These also are absent from the gatherings of the heretics and are a sign that the Christians are right in remaining in the apostolic Church.

Proving the Spirits

የ፦ የ፦ የ፦ የ፦ የ፦

4 1   Beloved, do not believe every spirit, but prove the spirits *to see* if they are from God; because many false-prophets have gone out into the world.

2   By this you know the Spirit of God: every spirit that confesses that Jesus Christ has come in the flesh is from God;

3   and every spirit that does not confess Jesus is not from God; and this is the *spirit* of the antichrist, of which you have heard that it is coming, and now it is already in the world.

4   You *yourselves* are from God, *little* children, and have conquered them; because greater is the One in you than the one in the world.

5   They are from the world; therefore they speak from the world, and the world hears them.

> 6 We *ourselves* are from God; the one knowing God hears us; the one who is not from God does not hear us. From this we know the spirit of truth and the spirit of deception.

Having mentioned the operations and gifts of the Spirit in the Church, St. John warns his **beloved** hearers of the possibility of false prophecies. The term **spirit** here refers to inspired utterances (compare 1 Cor. 14:12, where St. Paul uses the word with this meaning). There were at that time prophets in the churches, some of whom roamed from place to place. (A church manual called the *Didache*, or "Teaching," dating from about AD 100, would later deal with the issue of how to differentiate the true prophets from the false ones.) John warns his communities **not** to **believe every spirit** they hear or accept every utterance as genuine, **because many false-prophets have gone out into the world** and may show up at their assemblies. Instead, they must **prove** each utterance, testing *to see* **if they are from God.**

The criterion they are to use is that of Christological orthodoxy. They can recognize the genuine work of **the Spirit of God** by this: **every spirit that confesses that Jesus Christ has come in the flesh is from God; and every spirit that does not confess Jesus is not from God.** That is, if the prophecy (or prophet) in question confesses that Jesus is the Christ, and that He was truly incarnate in the flesh, they can be assured of its authenticity. Contrariwise, if the prophecy (or prophet) has a heretical view of Christ (such as those who deny the reality of Christ's Incarnation), they can be assured that it is counterfeit. Indeed, rather than just being a human error, this is **the *spirit* of the antichrist** operating. They have heard from the apostolic tradition that such demonic opposition is **coming** as a sign of the last time, and **now it is already in the world**. The last days have come. They must be on their guard.

Nonetheless, they need not fear, for they **are from God** (the pronoun is emphatic—contrasting to the false prophets) and **have conquered** the false prophets, unmasking them as the counterfeits they are (compare Rev. 2:2). This is only natural, **because greater**

189

is the One in them (God) **than the one in the world** (the devil).
Through God's help they will have no difficulty detecting false
prophecy, for they have been taught by His anointing (2:27).

These false prophets, though claiming to be of the Church, are
still **from the world** (which has the devil in it as its ruler). That is
why **they speak from the world** (saying, for example, that sinful
behavior is acceptable; compare 3:10), and **the world hears them**,
gladly accepting their message. How can the world not accept their
message, since they tell the world what it wants to hear and confirm
it in its sin? It is otherwise with the true Church. They (the pronoun
is again emphatic) **are from God** and tell the world to repent. Some
will heed the Church's message, and some will not, and from this
John's hearers can **know the spirit of truth and the spirit of deception**. The false prophets, animated by **the spirit of deception**, will
refuse to accept the message of the apostolic tradition.

Love One Another

℘ ℘ ℘ ℘ ℘

7   Beloved, let us love one another, because love is
    from God, and everyone loving has been born
    from God and knows God.

8   The one not loving does not know God, because
    God is love.

9   By this the love of God was manifested in us,
    that God has sent His only-begotten Son into
    the world that we might live through Him.

10 In this is love, not that we *ourselves* loved God,
    but that He *Himself* loved us, and sent His Son
    as the propitiation for our sins.

11 Beloved, if God loved us thus, we *ourselves* also
    ought to love one another.

12 No one has ever beheld God; if we love one
    another, God remains in us, and His love is
    perfected in us.

13 By this we know that we remain in Him and

> He in us, because He has given us of His Spirit.
>
> 14 And we *ourselves* have beheld and witness that the Father has sent the Son *as* the Savior of the world.
>
> 15 Whoever confesses that Jesus is the Son of God, God remains in him, and he in God.

As the true Church, those who are from God (v. 6), they must **love one another, because love is from God**, just as they are. **God is love** in His inmost nature, and so **everyone loving has been born *from God* and knows God**. To be born from God means to share His nature (as children share the nature of their parents), and God's nature is love—therefore, they, as His children, must love as God does.

By saying that **everyone loving has been born *from God***, John is not saying that even secular people who do not know Christ, but who act in a loving manner, have been born from God. Such people (if they indeed exist) are not here in John's view. He uses the inclusive term *everyone* (Gr. *pas*) to show that *every single Christian* who has truly been born of God must act in a loving manner. No Christian is exempt from this commandment: **the one not loving does not know God** and is no Christian at all.

John adds that **by this the love of God was manifested in us**, in the human race, **that God has sent His only-begotten Son into the world that we might live through Him**. St. John is not writing as a Greek philosopher when he says, "God is love." He is writing as an apostle and evangelist, proclaiming the Gospel. Love is always (by definition) manifested; it always reaches out to the beloved. One always loves someone or something else, for self-love is not love. And **the love of God was manifested** and made real in history in this—that He **has sent His only-begotten Son into the world.** The Incarnation of Christ is thus the expression and proof that God is love. We were all dead men, but Christ was sent **that we might live through Him** and be rescued from eternal death.

When we use the word "love," we are tempted to define it by our human expressions of love and make man the measure of all things. By "love," we therefore mean "love as we experience it from other people." This, says St. John, is totally inadequate to describe the nature of God. **In this is** true **love—not that we *ourselves* loved God, but that He *Himself* loved us** (the pronouns are both emphatic). We must define this love by God's astounding love for us, not our poor and paltry love for Him. For God did the astounding thing of **sending His Son *as* the propitiation for our sins**. The eternal Word of the Father, who was in the beginning with God (John 1:2), humbled Himself to share our poverty and even to die on the Cross in shame, darkness, and agony in order to offer the sacrifice that would reconcile us to the Father and give us life. *This* is the true measure of love and what John means when He says, "God is love."

John again states the result of this to his **beloved** children: **if God loved us thus**, in this way (Gr. *outos*), then **we *ourselves* also ought to love one another**. God valued and loved my brother enough to send His Son to die for him—how can I regard him with disdain and refuse to love him too? God is indeed the invisible God, for **no one has ever beheld God**. Nonetheless, **if we love one another, God remains in us**, and His invisible Presence is made real and manifested among us. His **love**, given to us, **is perfected in us** as it is given to our brother. The mutual love of the Christians therefore makes real and visible the Presence of the invisible God. God is seen in the world and by the world *through us* (compare John 13:35).

The apostle continues, **By this we know that we remain in Him and He in us, because He has given us of His Spirit**. That is, Christians can know the reality of this mutual indwelling of God in His people because of the presence of the Spirit in the Church. The Spirit (manifested in the Church through prophecies, healings, exorcisms, and other gifts) is only present where there is love. (Compare Wisdom 1:5; 7:27: "A holy and disciplined spirit will flee from deceit. . . . Wisdom passes into holy souls and makes them prophets.") Thus the presence of the Spirit's activity witnesses to the love of the brethren for one another.

As those who have received the Spirit, John (with the other apostles) speaks a prophetically authoritative word of **witness**, telling all men what they **have beheld**—namely, that **the Father has sent the Son** *as* **the Savior of the world**. The apostles (the **we** of v. 14 refers to them; compare 1:1–3), as God's true prophets and Spirit-filled witnesses, proclaim to all the truth about Jesus. Jesus is the true **Son** (compare the heretics' denial of this in 2:22–23), the One who died in the flesh as **the Savior of the world**. **Whoever believes this message and confesses that Jesus is the Son of God** comes to know God. **God remains in him, and he in God**. The loveless heretics have no share in this.

ॐ ॐ ॐ ॐ ॐ

16 And we *ourselves* have known and have believed the love which God has for us. God is love, and the one remaining in the love remains in God, and God remains in him.

17 By this the love has been perfected with us, that we may have boldness in the day of judgment; because as that One is, thus also are we *ourselves* in this world.

18 There is no fear in the love, but the perfect love casts the fear outside, because the fear has punishment, and the one fearing has not been perfected in the love.

19 We *ourselves* love, because He *Himself* first loved us.

20 If anyone says, "I love God," and hates his brother, he is a liar, for the one not loving his brother whom he has seen is not able to love God whom he has not seen.

21 And this commandment we have from Him, that the one loving God should love also his brother.

Those in the true Church (**we** *ourselves*; John classes himself with the rest of the believers) **have known and have believed the love which God has for us**. That is, they have experienced for themselves God's love through the love of their brothers, and now know how much God loves them. It is through this love of the brothers that the believer **remains in God, and God remains in him**, for to remain in the love is to remain in God, since **God is love**.

By this mutual love of the brothers, **love has been perfected with us**. God's love, planted in the believer's heart at his conversion, reaches its goal through this brotherly love. As a result, the believers **may have boldness in the day of judgment** and not fear that God will reject them, as He will the loveless heretics. The believer is like Jesus (**that One**, Gr. *ekeinos*), and as He is, **thus also are we *ourselves* in this world**. Jesus is righteous and loving, and since we are too, belonging not to the world, but to the Kingdom (John 17:14), we need have no fear on the Last Day.

That is because **there is no fear in the love, but the perfect love** (i.e. the perfected love of God that dwells in the brothers as brotherly love; vv. 12, 17) **casts the fear** completely **outside**. Fear and love are mutually exclusive. **Fear has punishment** as its focus, and since we know God's love for us, we know He will not punish us by rejecting us, as He will the unrighteous. **The one fearing** God and His wrath **has not been perfected in the love**. That one has not experienced God's love in all its heart-melting power through the love of the brothers.

John stresses that we have this love in our hearts only **because He *Himself* first loved us**. Our capacity to love, the transformation of our lives wherein we pass from death into life (3:14), is the result of God's prior love for us. God put His love in our hearts and changed us.

Such a change is absolutely necessary. **If anyone says, "I love God," and** yet **hates his brother, he is a liar**, and does not truly love God. In saying that **he is a liar**, John does not simply mean that he is telling a lie or is deluded. The term *liar* connects one with the devil, the father of lies (John 8:44; compare John's uses of the term in 2:22). The combination of pious claims and a heart full of hate reveals that the person is utterly opposed to God. Love for one's brother is an indispensable part of love for God. To **love his brother whom he has seen** is easier than **to love God whom he has**

not seen. If one can love and serve the invisible, then serving the visible should be no problem. A man who cannot love his brother, who stands before his eyes and who is like himself, is unlikely to be able to love God, whom no one has ever beheld (v. 12). We must, then, love our brother, for **this commandment we have from Him**. That is, God has commanded us to love our brother, so we cannot really love God without doing what He says. Thus **the one loving God should love also his brother**. Love for brother is inseparable from love for God.

ॐ ॐ ॐ ॐ ॐ

5 1   Everyone believing that Jesus is the Christ has been born from God; and everyone loving the one begetting loves the one born from him.

2   By this we know that we love the children of God, when we love God and do His commandments.

3   For this is the love of God, that we keep His commandments, and His commandments are not burdensome,

4   because everyone who has been born from God conquers the world; and this is the conquest that has conquered the world—our belief.

5   And who is the one conquering the world, but the one believing that Jesus is the Son of God?

John continues building on the thought of 4:21 in 5:1. **Everyone believing that Jesus is the Christ has been born from God; and everyone loving the one begetting** (i.e. the father) also **loves the one born from him** (i.e. the father's child). That is, if a man loves his own father, then he will love the father's other children as well. In this case, the other children of God our Father, the other ones **born from him**, are our fellow brothers in Christ, for they have **believed that Jesus is the Christ**, and thus also have **been born from**

God. If we love God, we must therefore love all our brothers too.

It is **by this we know that we love the children of God**, John says, **when we love God and do His commandments**. This last statement of verse 2 has caused some commentators problems. It seems to them that St. John is saying that the proof that we love our brothers is that we love God and do His commandments. This is odd, for John has been arguing the opposite—the proof that we love God is that we love our brothers, not *vice versa* (see 2:3; 4:20).

This, however, is to misunderstand John's words. He is not speaking in 5:2 of *how we know* that we love our brothers, but of *the identity of the true Church*. He does not say, "By this we know that we love *our brothers*," but rather, **by this we know that we love the children of God**. That those of John's communities love their brothers is not in question—either by them or anyone else. What is in question is the *status* of those people—are they deluded (as John's opponents, the heretics, say), or are they the true children of God? In short, which of the two groups—John's communities or the schismatics—are the true children of God? John says that it is by this that one may know that—the ones who **love God** and **do His commandments** are the true **children of God**. The heretics opposing John's message have no claim to be God's true children, for they do not keep His commandments, but live in sinful immorality.

John adds that to **love God** and to **keep His commandments** are inextricably linked, for if we love someone, we delight to do as he asks. This is all the more so, since **His commandments are not burdensome**. God has not required us to do extraordinary ascetic exploits, or to attain the unscaled heights of philosophical wisdom. He has simply required that we believe in the Name of Jesus His Son and love one another (3:23). That is within the reach of the humblest disciple of Jesus.

Indeed, **everyone who has been born from God** can do this, for he **conquers the world**. This **conquest** [Gr. *nike*] **that has conquered** [Gr. *nikao*] **the world** refers to the Christian's victory over all the lies, half-truths, and heresies the world throws at him, and finding his way to God and truth. None of the devil's lies or heresies can separate him from God, for he overcomes all through his **belief**, his faith (Gr. *pistis*; cognate with *pisteuo*, "to believe"). Fervent belief in Christ is all that is needed to sustain us and give us victory over the opposition of the world. As long as we hold to this, we conquer all (compare Rev. 2:7, with its refrain, "to him who conquers"). John triumphantly asks, **who is** able to do this, to **conquer the world**? Surely, only **the one believing** [Gr. *pisteuo*] **that Jesus is the Son of God**. Only the one who holds to the apostolic witness has the faith that gives final victory on the Last Day.

Testimony to Christ

6 This One is the One who came through water and blood, Jesus Christ, not with the water only, but with the water and with the blood.

7 And the Spirit is the One witnessing, because the Spirit is the truth,

8 because there are three that are witnessing, the Spirit and the water and the blood; and the three are for the one *truth*.*

9 If we receive the witness of men, the witness of God is greater, because this is the witness of God, that He has witnessed about His Son.

10 The one believing in the Son of God has the witness in himself; the one not believing God has made Him a liar, because he has not believed in the witness that God has witnessed about His Son.

11 And this is the witness, that God has given us eternal life, and this life is in His Son.

12 The one having the Son has the life; the one not having the Son of God does not have the life.

* *The reading that speaks of the Father, the Word, and the Spirit in heaven is not authentic; it appears in no Greek manuscript before the fourteenth century, and is quoted by no Father writing at the time of the Christological controversies, for whom such a verse would have been helpful.*

St. John elaborates on this apostolic witness and what it means to "believe in the Son of God" (v. 5). **This One**, the true Son of God, is the One who **came through water and blood, Jesus Christ, not with the water only, but with the water and with the blood**. The heretics (like Cerinthus) asserted that Christ came only with water, in that the Christ-spirit descended on the human Jesus at His Baptism, but departed from Jesus before the blood of the Cross. Thus in their teaching Jesus was not "Jesus Christ," for the Christ-spirit was separate from Jesus. Against such lies, John counters that the Son of God **came through** both **water and blood**, in that Christ experienced both the water of baptism and the blood of crucifixion and death. He was truly **Jesus Christ**, for Jesus *was* the Christ, not simply a carrier of the Christ-spirit for a while. **And the Spirit is the One witnessing** to the truth of these things. How could He not?—for **the Spirit is the truth** itself, and these things are true.

The reference to **the Spirit** (as with other references to the Spirit in 3:24; 4:2, 13) probably refers to prophetic gifts in the church assembly. John reminds his hearers that the prophetic utterances they have heard confirm that Jesus is the Christ, and that He died on the Cross for the salvation of the world (compare 4:2).

Thus **there are three that are witnessing** (and three witnesses are all that are needed to prove a case; Deut. 19:15), and these three **are for the one** *truth*, all alike pointing to the same thing. These three are **the Spirit and the water and the blood**. All alike witness that Jesus is the Son of God.

The Spirit does this through the prophecies of the Christian assemblies, for the prophets speaking them bring this confession of faith. **The water** of baptism continues to witness to this, for the circumstances of Jesus' Baptism confirm Him as the Son of God. When He was baptized, the Spirit descended on Him as a dove, and the Voice of the Father called Him His beloved Son (Mark 1:10–11). **The blood** of His Cross also witnesses that He is the Son of God. The circumstances of His death, no less than His Baptism, show His divinity. He did not die as other men do, involuntarily and helpless before death. Rather, as God He sovereignly cried, "It is finished!" bowed His head, and delivered up His spirit (John 19:30). He died as One who had complete control, and death came to Him only when it was called.

All of this confirms that Jesus is the Christ, the Son of God (compare John 20:31). All receive **the witness of men**, and the consistent testimony of three witnesses is sufficient to prove a case. How much more, when we have **the witness of God**, which is **greater** than the witness of men? Through all these three things, **He has witnessed about His Son**, speaking through the Christian prophets, speaking and sending the Spirit at Christ's Baptism, and giving Him authority over death at His Cross.

The one believing in the Son of God and accepting that witness **has the witness in himself**. The believer has internalized God's witness and made it his own. He now knows firsthand the truth of what God has said (compare the internal anointing of 2:27) and can discern truth from falsehood. **The one not believing God** (that is, rejecting the apostolic teaching about Jesus; note the equation of the Church's witness with God's witness) **has made** God **a liar**. The heretics claim to represent God's deeper teaching, but in fact they *mis*represent God by (in effect) saying that He lies, since they **have not believed in the witness that God has witnessed about His Son** through the Spirit's work and the facts of Christ's Baptism and death. John writes with great irony. The heretics claim that Jesus is not the Christ, and God says that Jesus *is* the Christ—obviously, then, the heretics must think that God is lying!

God's **witness** and the Church's message, St. John says, may be summed up like this: **God has given us eternal life**. By **eternal life**, John means Jesus Christ, for **this life is in His Son**. God **has given us eternal life** in that He sent Jesus Christ to bring us that life (the verb rendered *has given*, Gr. *edoken*, is in the aorist tense, indicating the once-for-all event of the Incarnation). John thus returns to what he said in 1:2, saying that in Jesus the eternal life of God is manifested on the earth.

That means that **the one having the Son** and abiding in the true Church **has the life**, while **the one not having the Son of God** (by rejecting the Church's teaching) **does not have the life**. In denying life to the heretics, there is no arbitrariness or unfairness. Eternal life is only to be found in the Son of God, so to reject Him is to be without life—not as a result of God's arbitrary judgment, but as the logical consequence of one's choice. The choice between the apostolic message and heresy is stark indeed, with eternal consequences. Let none of John's flock, therefore, defect from the message they have received!

§III.   Conclusion (5:13–21)

> ৪৩ ৪৩ ৪৩ ৪৩ ৪৩
>
> 13 These *things* I have written to you, that you may know that you have eternal life, to those believing in the Name of the Son of God.
> 14 And this is the boldness which we have before Him, that, if we ask anything according to His will, He hears us.
> 15 And if we know that He hears us in whatever we ask, we know that we have requests which we have asked from Him.

St. John now begins to conclude his letter, saying, **these *things* I have written to you, that you may know that you have eternal life, to those believing in the Name of the Son of God**. He writes to warn them of the danger of defecting to the heretical schismatics, and of being seduced by their claims to represent a deeper teaching. They may be unsure that they should stay where they are, and so John wants them to **know** that they already **have eternal life**, since they **believe in the Name of the Son of God**. Unlike the heretics, they have **believed** that Jesus is the Christ, **the Son of God**, and have accepted that orthodox proclamation of the Savior. They are safe where they are.

As part of the true Church, they **have boldness** of approach **before Him**, so that **if** they can **ask anything according to His will, He hears** them. (The requests are said to be **according to His will**, for prayer is not a blunt instrument for coercing God to do *our* will, but our privileged share in doing *His* will.) This authority in prayer, this privileged access to God, is only given to those who call upon **the Name of the Son of God** as His true Church. The schismatics have no share in this holy access given only to His children.

John speaks of God granting our **requests which we have asked from Him**. I would suggest that (as in 3:22) the context is liturgical, not individual, and John is not speaking so much about individual believers asking God for things in prayer, but of the church assembly standing before God and petitioning Him. The **requests**, therefore, are primarily those things for which the Church asks God in their common prayers: forgiveness, grace, strength, healing. John is not here giving a *carte blanche* to individuals to get from God their personal wish lists. He is reassuring the Church of their status as God's chosen people, His royal priesthood, with unhindered access to the King.

☙ ☙ ☙ ☙ ☙

16 If anyone sees his brother sinning a sin not *leading* to death, he will ask and He will give life to him, to those who sin not *leading* to death. There is a sin *leading* to death; about that *sin* I do not say that you should ask.

17 Every unrighteousness is sin, and there is a sin not *leading* to death.

Part of this unhindered access and authority before God is the authority to reconcile penitents, to ask for and get forgiveness for those who have strayed into sin, and who now return to the saving path of righteousness.

Thus **if anyone sees his brother sinning** (note: the term *brother* denotes a Christian), **he will ask and** God **will give life** to the erring and penitent brother. (These sins, we may think, are not the daily ones of minor impatience, laziness, or lust, but more obvious and grave offenses—distressing events, not inner temptations, for a brother can **see** the sinner committing it.)

The brother asking for life for the sinner is asking in the midst of the liturgical assembly, voicing the prayer of the assembled Church, for authority to bring God's forgiveness is given to the Church, not to every Christian in it (see John 20:22–23). Once again, the context is liturgical.

John adds that the sin involved must be **a sin not *leading* to death**. Admittedly, **every unrighteousness is sin**—John is not saying that some unrighteousness and evil is acceptable! But not all sin is **sin *leading* to death**, and it is about this latter sin that he **does not say that** they **should ask**. His promise that God will forgive sin and give life does not hold good for this sin.

What is this **sin *leading* to death**? It is the sin committed in schism, the sin of one who has fallen from the faith into the apostasy of the heretics. In speaking of the sinning brother being given life, John refers to the sins of Christians being forgiven through the Blood of Christ in the Church's eucharistic worship (1:7, 9). Those sins, John says, are forgiven by God as the Church prays for us. But since the schismatic has separated himself from the Church, the grace of eucharistic prayer is unavailing for him and cannot heal this sin. Eucharistic grace indeed flows to all in the Church, but these sinners have separated themselves from the Church—and therefore from its healing grace.

ॐ ॐ ॐ ॐ ॐ

18 We know that no one who has been born from God sins; but the One who was born from God keeps him, and the Evil One does not touch him.

19 We know that we are from God, and the whole world lies in the Evil One.

20 And we know that the Son of God has come and has given us insight, that we might know the True *One*, and we are in the True *One*, in His Son Jesus Christ. This One is the true God and eternal life.

21 *Little* children, guard yourselves from the idols.

John finishes his epistle with three reminders to help his hearers resist heretical error, telling them once more of what they already **know** and have been taught in the apostolic tradition.

Firstly, John says they **know that no one who has been born from God sins; but the One who was born from God keeps him**, so that **the Evil One does not touch him**. John here repeats what he said in 3:6f. The true believer does not live a life of sin. He strives to please God and does not embrace a lifestyle hateful to God. When he lives as God's child, **the One who was born from God keeps him**.

Both the believer and Jesus are described here as **born from God**, and John intends to show by this the union of the believer with Christ. That is, Christ keeps the believer safe because the believer has been born from God and is also God's child. (Obviously, however, there is a difference, for Christ is the eternal Son by nature, and the believer is the adopted son by grace. Yet Christ is still the Firstborn among many brothers; Rom. 8:29.) Christ keeps safe the Father's other children.

This "keeping," however, must be carefully examined. John does *not* say that Christ keeps the believer from sinning. If that were so, how could it be that any believer would ever sin (as we know they do)? And if he did, would it not then be Christ's fault for not keeping him from sinning?

Rather, Christ **keeps** the believer in that He keeps him safe from **the Evil One**, so that the enemy **does not touch him**. The thought is the same as in John 17:12, 15, where Christ says that He keeps His disciples from the Evil One. "To keep" is here the opposite of "to lose," and Christ keeps His own in that He will lose none of those who entrust themselves to Him in faith and righteousness (John 6:39). The enemy, for all his cunning, lies, and persecution, will not be able to touch or harm Christ's holy disciples, so long as they walk in the light (2:10). This does not mean, of course, that apostasy is impossible, as if Christ's keeping overrides the believer's free will. It does mean that so long as the believer trusts in Christ, he will never be lost.

Secondly, John says that they **know that** they **are from God**, and that **the whole world lies in the Evil One**, buried under his power. The Evil One rules this world (John 14:30), pulling the strings, spreading his lies, and holding men in his thrall of deception and sin and death. The true Church, however, lies outside his power, and those remaining in her bosom are safe. The Church is the beacon of light in a land of darkness, an island of truth in a sea of lies. John's hearers must remain in this haven.

Thirdly, John says that they **know that the Son of God has come and has given** them **insight**. This reference to Jesus as **the Son of God** contains another hidden reference to the heretics, who deny that He is the Son of God (compare 4:15). The heretics claim a superior insight, but John says that it is those of the apostolic Church who have the real **insight**.

This insight consists of the experiential knowledge of the True God. It is in the apostolic church alone that men come to **know the True *One*** (compare John 17:3), for all the world lies in error (v. 19). Moreover, through God's grace, they are **in the True *One***, abiding safely in God (4:15), and this is because they are also **in His Son Jesus Christ**. To abide in God means also to abide in Jesus, for it is through our discipleship to Christ that we experience the Father.

In saying this, John reaches his climax. His hearers are already **in the True *One*** and **in His Son**, and should resist any temptations to defect. Jesus (**this One**, emphatic, Gr. *outos*) **is the true God and eternal life**. Christ, as well as the Father, is **the true God** (John 1:1), the One through whom the Father is manifest in the world (John 14:9). He is also eternal life (1 John 1:2). To leave Christ (that is, the apostolic Church) is thus to leave God and eternal life.

Having come to know the True God, they must, John exhorts his *little* **children**, **guard** themselves **from the idols**. By **the idols**, John does not mean pagan images or statues, such as were used for the worship of the Greek gods. He means anything other than the true God—in this case, the false gods proffered by the heretics. To accept their false version of Jesus is to accept an idol—something every bit as heathen as the images standing mute in the pagan temples. St. John urges his hearers to stay far from such falsities and to guard themselves from them by remaining steadfastly in their holy apostolic faith.

❧ The Second Epistle of St. John ❧

Introduction

In this second epistle, St. John writes with the heart of a shepherd to one of the churches under his pastoral oversight—probably one of the seven churches of Asia. One of those churches was especially menaced by the heretical teaching against which John wrote his first epistle, and he writes this present letter to warn them against receiving visitors bringing that teaching.

There is no way to know whether this letter was written before or after the first epistle, despite its having come down to us as the so-called second epistle. The enumeration of these letters is not based on anything in the letters themselves. Similarly, the date is impossible to decide with accuracy. If the first epistle was written about AD 85, this present letter might date from about the same time, since the heresy John here warns of seems to be the same, with no further developments.

The neighboring church to which John was writing is presented under the metaphor of a gracious lady (Gr. *kuria*, feminine of *kurios*, "lord"). This is because all the churches are spiritually feminine, being the bride of Christ (see also Rev. 21:2), and all churches are considered as sister churches.

Also, the use of metaphor might be a precaution against persecution. If the letter was indeed written about AD 85, persecution was heating up against the churches of Asia. The use of metaphor might be a deliberate attempt to hide from prying eyes both the identity of the church sending the letter (probably the church in Ephesus, where John resided) and the identity of the church receiving the letter, lest either community be persecuted by the pagan authorities. This might also account for the complete lack of personal names in this epistle.

There is also no way to determine which church it was sent to.

I would suggest (very tentatively) the church in Smyrna. Smyrna was near to Ephesus (it is mentioned second in the list of the seven churches of Asia in Rev. 2—3; see Rev. 2:8f), and it experienced persecution, for Christ warns this church in Revelation 2:10 that they are to experience more tribulation for a time. If persecution was a factor in the letter's use of metaphor and lack of names, Smyrna is a suitable candidate.

Also, Polycarp, the second-century bishop of Smyrna, vividly preserved the memory of John, for he knew him personally (see St. Irenaeus, *Against Heresies*, 3, 3, 4). This may reflect particularly warm and close relations between John and the church of Smyrna.

Whatever the epistle's exact destination, it was received by the Church (after some hesitation) as the genuine work of John, the Beloved Disciple, and treasured accordingly.

❧ The Second Epistle of St. John ❧

§I. Opening Greetings (1–3)

❧ ❧ ❧ ❧ ❧

1 The elder to the chosen lady and her children, whom I *myself* love in truth; and not only I myself, but also all those who have known the truth,

2 because of the truth remaining in us and *which* will be with us forever;

3 Grace, mercy, peace will be with us, from God the Father and from Jesus Christ, the Son of the Father, in truth and love.

St. John calls himself **the elder** (Gr. *presbuteros*)—literally, "the old man." It would seem this was an affectionate title for the apostle.

Papias, a bishop in Asia Minor in about AD 130 (quoted by Eusebius in his *Church History*, 3, 39), wrote about "the elders' discourses, what was said by Andrew, Peter, Philip, Thomas, James, John, Matthew, or any other of the Lord's disciples." He also mentions "what Aristion and the elder John say," implying that these were then still living. It would seem that the term "elder" denoted one of the first generation, a usage perhaps going back to John himself.

John writes **to the chosen lady and her children, whom I *myself* love in truth**. As mentioned above, the term *lady* (Gr. *kuria*) is a metaphor for the local church there, it being the bride of the Lord (Gr. *kurios*). **Her children** are the actual members of the community. John affirms that these he **loves in truth**. That is, he loves them in the **truth** of the Gospel (not just "truly loves them"), for "truth" is one of those theologically loaded words in

John's writings. John says that he loves them for their devotion to the truth of the Gospel, a devotion that clings to that truth despite all temptations to apostasy. This interpretation is confirmed by his adding, **and not only I myself, but also all those who have known the truth**. All the Christians in the area who have known the truth of the apostolic faith also love and admire this community for its persevering loyalty.

John writes his letter **because of the truth remaining in** them, **and *which* will be with** them **forever**. He writes to preserve them in the eternal **truth** which already is **remaining in** them, and **which will be with** them **forever**, leading them from earth to heaven, from this world into the world to come. The truth, though eternal in itself, now needs safeguarding from the lies and distortions of the heretics.

This truth becomes **grace, mercy,** and **peace** in their midst once it has been accepted by them, and that is why John uses these words as the conventional opening greeting for his letter. He writes, **the truth . . . will be with us . . . grace, mercy, peace will be with us,** putting the two realities of **truth** and **grace, mercy, peace** in apposition because the first reality produces the second.

This reality and blessing of grace, mercy, and peace comes **from God the Father and from Jesus Christ, the Son of the Father**. John pairs **God the Father** and **Jesus Christ** because of their unity, for the Father is known through knowing the Son. The very title **Jesus Christ** is significant here, for John is warning against heretics who deny that Jesus is the Christ (1 John 2:22). Jesus is called **the Son of the Father** for the same reason, to assert His deity against the heretics who would deny it. The blessings of **grace, mercy,** and **peace** will come to the church through the Father and the Son, but only if the church members abide **in truth and love**. To defect from the **truth** or to refuse to walk in **love** would be to forfeit their share in God's life.

§II.　　Warnings against Antichrists (4–11)

ॐ ॐ ॐ ॐ ॐ

4　I rejoiced exceedingly that I have found *some* of your children walking in truth, as we have

> received commandment from the Father.
>
> 5 And now I ask you, lady, not as writing a new commandment to you, but that which we have had from the beginning, that we should love one another.
>
> 6 And this is the love, that we should walk according to His commandments. This is the commandment, as you have heard from the beginning, that you should walk in it,
>
> 7 because many deceivers have gone out into the world, those who do not confess Jesus Christ *as* coming in the flesh. This one is the deceiver and the antichrist.

John now comes to the purpose of his epistle. He **found *some* of** their **children walking in truth,** preserving the orthodox apostolic faith, just as they **received commandment from the Father** through Jesus. The faith in the divine Son of God which Jesus gave to His Church is kept unaltered by them.

These **children** are members of the neighboring community who came to visit John. As heresy continued to spread, John **rejoiced** to see them untouched by it, keeping the commandment of the Father (v. 4). He is sending them back home with this epistle, **asking** those of their church (the **lady**) to keep another commandment as well—to **love one another**. They have the faith; in the face of the heresy that is spreading loveless pride and sowing disunity, they need to take care to preserve love also. In **writing** this, John stresses, he is not teaching unheard-of novelties (as the heretics do). This is **not a new commandment**, but **that which** they **have had from the beginning** of their experience in Christ. This is no innovation, but a return to basics.

Moreover, the commandment to love is a part of the commandment to have faith in Jesus. For John adds, **this is the love**, this is the implication of that love—that they **should walk according to His commandments, the commandment** they **have heard from the beginning, that** they **should walk in it**. What is this

commandment (singular, v. 6b) which they **heard from the beginning** as the basis for their Christian life (**that** they **should walk in it**)? It is the **commandment** mentioned in verse 4, which the **children** of the neighboring church are **walking in**—the commandment to "believe in the Name of His Son Jesus Christ" (compare 1 John 3:23), the commandment to hold to the truth. The **commandments** (plural; v. 6a) are all the teachings of Christ He gave to the apostles as the word of His Father. That is, love of the brothers implies orthodoxy of belief, for truth and love are inextricably bound together in the Christian life.

John urgently needs to exhort them to keep this commandment, **because many deceivers have gone out into the world, those who do not confess Jesus Christ *as* coming in the flesh**. These traveling preachers do not keep this commandment. They assert that Jesus is not the Christ, but that the Christ-spirit descended on Him at His baptism and left Him before His death. According to them, Christ was therefore not truly incarnate and had not **come in the flesh**. The influence of these men makes the original Christological teaching (the commandment from the Father; v. 4) all the more important. The traveling preacher is not a bringer of deeper truth, as he claims; **this one is the deceiver and the antichrist**, long expected.

🙞 🙞 🙞 🙞 🙞

8 Watch out *for* yourselves, lest you lose what we have worked *for*, but that you might receive a full reward.

9 Everyone who goes on ahead and not remaining in the teaching of the Christ does not have God; the one who remains in the teaching, this one has both the Father and the Son.

10 If anyone comes to you and does not bring this teaching, do not receive him into your house, and do not say to him, "Greetings!"

11 for the one saying to him, "Greetings!" shares in his evil works.

Because of this, John's hearers must **watch out**, lest they **lose what** they **have worked** *for* and accomplished and forfeit the **full reward** of eternal life that is promised them. By their perseverance in the truth and love, they have stored up for themselves a great reward. Let them take care not to be seduced by these men, lest they receive nothing for all their labors!

The word rendered *work for* is the Greek *ergazomai*, cognate with *ergon*, "work." Their work is the work of faith (compare John 6:29) and its manifestation through righteousness and love (1 John 3:10). John uses the word *ergazomai* here to stress how much they have accomplished, and how great will be their loss if they defect to the schismatics. He himself is not uninvolved in this work, for the most likely manuscript reading is, **what we have worked** *for* (not, "what *you* have worked for"). John himself, who proclaims the faith and cares for the Christians of Asia Minor pastorally, also works for their salvation and reward, and he too would be grieved to see it done in vain.

They can be sure of this: **everyone who goes on ahead**, **not remaining in the teaching of the Christ** that was delivered to them, **does not have God** any longer. The heretics claim to present more advanced lessons about God. Every single person who leaves the apostolic teaching about Christ and accepts these "advanced lessons" will not only not have more of God's truth—they will not have God at all. This teaching does not just present a false Christ; it presents a false view of God the Father also, so that the heretic has no divine truth whatsoever. **The one who remains in the teaching** he has received, this one will not just retain the truth about Christ, he will continue to **have both the Father and the Son**.

So, **if anyone comes** to their house churches, or seeks to be a part of their eucharistic gatherings, or seeks hospitality while traveling, and **does not bring this teaching** of the apostles, the faithful should **not receive him into** the **house**. They should not even **say to him, "Greetings!"** (the mildest of salutations), thereby acknowledging him as a fellow Christian. **The one saying to him, "Greetings!"** and welcoming him **shares in his evil works**. By granting them hospitality or allowing them eucharistic fellowship (the weekly sign of accepting their teaching), the tolerant one would be giving the heretic a credibility he does not deserve, and thus furthering his antichristian works. These **works** are **evil** and of the Evil One, and will be punished by God. If the faithful do not want God to punish them, too, let them discern between truth and heresy and refuse to acknowledge these men as fellow believers.

§III. Closing Words (12–13)

ॐ ॐ ॐ ॐ ॐ

12 Having many *things* to write to you, I do not intend *to do so* through paper and ink, but I hope to be with you and speak face to face, that our joy may be fulfilled.
13 The children of your chosen sister greet you.

Having warned them of the danger of falling from orthodoxy, John concludes his brief letter. The brevity of the note, however, does not mean he has nothing else to say to his beloved sister church. He has **many *things* to write** to them, but does **not intend *to do so* through paper and ink**. Rather, such is his love for them that he **hopes to be with** them **and speak face to face** (lit., "mouth to mouth"), exchanging words in the close intimacy of physical presence. That way, his own **joy** will **be fulfilled** (compare 1 John 1:4), for his joy depends on their joy and well-being.

He ends by speaking for his own community, saying, **the children of** their **chosen sister greet** them. All the faithful are interconnected, and those of John's own church send their greetings and love to their orthodox neighbors.

❧ The Third Epistle of St. John ❧

Introduction

As the proverb has it, "The more things change, the more they stay the same." Power struggles, which mar the church to this day, are nothing new, and even John the Apostle had to deal with them.

It appears that there was opposition to John's leadership in Asia, and that Diotrephes (almost certainly a presbyter) was the ringleader of it (v. 9). It may seem surprising to some that there was opposition to an apostle. But this epistle, like the other epistles of John, was written perhaps about AD 85, and John was by this time quite elderly. I would suggest that some, like Diotrephes, sympathized with the new gnostic teaching spreading in the area and objected to John's condemnation of it. John's opposition was perhaps portrayed as the outdated misgivings of an old man—a dear old man, of course, and an apostle, but after all, one who was out of touch with the way of the world. The Church must not be held captive to John's blind conservatism, Diotrephes perhaps argued, and for its own sake must become progressive. John, dear old man that he was, must be firmly set aside.

I would suggest that Diotrephes refused to recognize the messengers John sent to counteract the spread of the new gnostic teaching (v. 10). Though not yet committed to this teaching (John does not denounce him as a heretic), Diotrephes perhaps had a growing sympathy for it and thought that John was wrong to oppose it so firmly. Certainly John, in commending Gaius and Demetrius (vv. 3, 12), stresses their loyalty to the truth (i.e. to his own rejection of the spreading heresy).

John intended to come and deal decisively with the rebellion of Diotrephes (v. 10). In preparation for this, he was sending Demetrius (probably the bearer of his epistle) to his friend Gaius. Gaius may have lived in a village somewhat outside the city where Diotrephes lived. He had been ill (v. 2), and may for this reason have been out of touch with recent events there. John urges Gaius to welcome Demetrius and those with him (v. 8). They were coming to form a beachhead for John, so that he could come later and deal with the problem. It is possible that Demetrius asked to be commended by name in this epistle (v. 12) because he was one of those who were expelled by Diotrephes, and he wanted this specific commendation from the apostle to fortify him as he returned to the place from which he had been expelled.

The letter remains in the Church as a testimony to the difficulties that often beset us. We should not despair when we encounter such things, for even the Beloved Disciple himself had to endure them.

❧ The Third Epistle of St. John ❧

§I.   **Opening Greetings (1–4)**

ॐ ॐ ॐ ॐ ॐ

1   The elder to the beloved Gaius, whom I *myself*
    love in truth.
2   Beloved, about all *things* I pray you may prosper
    and be in health, just as your soul prospers.
3   For I rejoiced exceedingly when brothers came
    and witnessed of you *being* in truth, just as you
    yourself are walking in truth.
4   I have no greater joy than these *things*, to hear
    of my children walking in the truth.

As in his second epistle, John refers to himself by the affectionate title by which he was known to the churches of Asia Minor, **the
elder**, "the old man" (see comments on 2 John 1). He writes to the
beloved Gaius, whom he loves in truth.

As stated above, **Gaius** possibly resides in a village near the town
where Diotrephes, the ringleader of the opposition, lives. John **loves**
him, rejoicing in his loyalty to the **truth**, that is, his fidelity to the
apostolic Gospel and his resistance to the gnostic heresy that is
spreading in the area. John addresses Gaius tenderly as his **beloved**
friend and **prays** that in **all** *things* Gaius might **prosper and be
in health**, so that his body enjoys the same health as his **soul**. It
seems that Gaius has been ill (and perhaps this is why he is not
current with events nearby, and needs John to tell him of them).
John not only wishes his friend to be in health because he loves
him, but also because he is sending a visitor to him (Demetrius,
the bearer of the letter) and will later come himself, and he has

217

no desire to burden a sick man with the demands of hospitality.

The word rendered *prosper* is the Greek *euodoo*, literally, "to have a good road," from the words *eu* ("good") and *odos* ("way, road"). The prosperity or success John wishes for his friend is that of unimpeded progress to health (Paul uses the same verb in Rom. 1:10, where it describes his desire to make his way safely to Rome). Financial prosperity is not here in view.

John is confident that Gaius's **soul prospers** and that he is progressing spiritually because **brothers came** to him from Gaius and **witnessed** to John of how Gaius was **in** the **truth**, and that he, for one (the pronoun is emphatic), was **walking in truth**. That is, they enthused about the loving welcome they received from him and about how he was making ever more spiritual progress—not just *being* **in** the truth, but **walking** in it, making his way without obstacle.

John **rejoiced exceedingly** to hear such things. As a faithful spiritual father, he has **no greater joy** than to **hear** of his spiritual **children walking in the truth** and prospering in their souls, as he heard that Gaius was doing.

§II.   Warning against Diotrephes (5–12)

Gaius Commended

🐿 🐿 🐿 🐿 🐿

5   Beloved, you are doing a faithful *thing* whenever you work for the brothers, and especially strangers;

6   who witness of your love before the church; whom you will do well to send forth *in a manner* worthy of God.

7   For they went out for the Name, receiving nothing from the Gentiles.

8   Therefore we *ourselves* ought to take up such *men*, that we may become co-workers with the truth.

St. John commends his **beloved** Gaius for the **faithful *thing*** he is **doing whenever** he **works for** the visiting **brothers**. (The word *whenever* indicates that Gaius did this many times.) This work is **especially** praiseworthy when the visiting brothers are **strangers** and not known to him, for then he welcomes them in simply because they claim to be fellow Christians. In saying that this is **a faithful *thing***, John probably means that by these acts Gaius shows that he is faithful to God—and to John (unlike Diotrephes).

The word rendered *work for* is the Greek *ergazomai*, used also in 2 John 8. The thought is of Gaius doing a work (Gr. *ergon*, cognate with *ergazomai*) and accomplishing a great labor of love. Gaius took the strangers in, gave them food and shelter as they traveled, washed their clothes, and sent them on their way in peace, probably with extra provisions. A labor indeed! When these brothers returned, they **witnessed** of his **love before** their whole home **church**. John says that Gaius **will do well to send** such men **forth *in a manner* worthy of** the **God** they serve. (By saying, **you will do well**, John means, "Please keep doing it.") God provides His servants with all they need, and Gaius he urges to do likewise.

This is all the more fitting, **for they went out for the Name** of Jesus, **receiving nothing from the Gentiles**. In their traveling missions undertaken for Jesus' sake, they did not beg for support from the pagans or stay with them. They did not want to be perceived as in their debt, nor be open to accusation that they were like the traveling philosophers and other religious charlatans, who abused people's hospitality and supported themselves by begging. (St. Paul too was keen to avoid such criticism; see 1 Cor. 9:1ff.) John says that all of them (the **we** is emphatic) **ought to take up** and support **such *men***, that they **may become co-workers with the truth**. By supporting and offering hospitality to these men, all the believers might have a share in their work and support the cause of **the truth**. This means they will also share in the reward.

In commending this work of hospitality, John is not speaking in the abstract. Diotrephes did not offer these men hospitality, because they came from John. Gaius is commended for doing what

Diotrephes refused to do. It is possible that they came to Gaius after they had been refused hospitality by Diotrephes.

Diotrephes Denounced

ॐ ॐ ॐ ॐ ॐ

9 I wrote something to the church, but the one loving to be first *among* them, Diotrephes, does not welcome us in.

10 For this *reason*, if I come, I will remind *them of* his works which he does, *accusingly* gossiping *about* us with evil words, and not satisfied with these *things*, he himself neither welcomes in the brothers, and he forbids those who intend *to do so*, and casts them out from the church.

11 Beloved, do not imitate what is evil, but what is good. The one doing good is from God; the one doing evil has not seen God.

12 Demetrius has been witnessed to by everyone, and by the truth itself; and we *ourselves* also witness, and you know that our witness is true.

The apostle says that he **wrote something to the church** (probably the church of Diotrephes), but **Diotrephes** (a leading presbyter there) **does not welcome us in**. Rather, he rejects John's authority and will not give hospitality to John's messengers or let them read his letter to the church.

It is not clear what this letter was. It is possible that it was John's first epistle, but if that were so, one might have expected John to phrase his indignation at the letter's rejection in more doctrinal terms, since that epistle was exclusively concerned with doctrine. If Diotrephes refused to let John's messengers read 1 John, it would have signaled his alignment with the heresy in no uncertain terms. Though (we have suggested) Diotrephes' quarrel with the apostle is in part rooted in his growing sympathy for the heresy, it is clear he has not yet declared himself in favor of it. John censures him for his lust for power, not for outright heresy.

So, we can only guess at the letter's contents. Perhaps John wrote them to receive the messengers he was sending with his exhortation to resist heresy. In that case, the letter is now lost, doubtless because Diotrephes had it destroyed. Perhaps John simply wrote that they should refuse hospitality to visitors bringing heretical teaching, and did not mention sending any visitors of his own. If that were so, it is possible that the letter survives as 2 John. Whatever the letter's contents and fate, Diotrephes refused it.

Diotrephes is introduced (in the Greek text, which gives his name only after the unflattering description) as **the one loving to be first** *among* **them**. This is the English rendering of the Greek participle of the verb *philoproteuo*, literally "first-place loving." The image is of one who always wants to be preeminent, one with a lust for power, one who loves to dominate. The church there was persuaded to repudiate John's messengers, and Diotrephes was leading this revolt.

John is planning to **come** and deal with this situation. He will bring all of Diotrephes' secret slander to light and let all the faithful know of his behind-the-scenes outrages. He will **remind** the gathered assembly of Diotrephes' **works which he does** unceasingly—how he *accusingly* **gossips** *about* John **with evil words**, how he **neither welcomes in the brothers** John sends, how he **forbids those who intend** to welcome them, and even **casts them out from the church**.

John's words give a clear picture of Diotrephes' strategy. Diotrephes is *accusingly* **gossiping** about John **with evil words**. The word translated *accusingly gossip* is the Greek *phluareo*. It is cognate with the word used in 1 Timothy 5:13, where it describes the malicious gossip of busybody women. Diotrephes is bad-mouthing the apostle, spreading **evil words** as gossip, perhaps saying how out of touch John is and unfit to lead. This is not outright repudiation of John's authority, but a sneaky smear campaign aimed at setting him aside.

Not satisfied with indirect attack, Diotrephes refuses to **welcome in** John's messengers (the verb rendered *welcome in* is the same verb used in v. 9: Diotrephes will receive neither John's letter nor his friends). He will not give them hospitality, nor an opportunity to read their letter or to speak for themselves. Further, he **forbids those who intend** *to do so*, intimidating them and **casting them out from the church**. Doubtless on trumped-up charges, Diotrephes had those who would give hospitality to John's people excommunicated and refused eucharistic fellowship themselves.

All of this is behind the scenes, and perhaps unknown to many of the rank and file—which is why John plans to **remind** everyone of it when he comes and bring it all out in the open. For now, he exhorts his beloved Gaius **not** to **imitate** such **evil, but what is good**. Gaius, of course, does not need such an exhortation, but John is writing with an eye to those who will read the epistle after him. John writes not only to encourage his friend Gaius, but also to strike the first counter-blow against Diotrephes by addressing the community through his advance letter.

Thus he writes that **the one doing good is from God**; whereas **the one doing evil has not seen God** at all. This assertion (v. 11b) may seem like a truism, but it is not. **Doing good** is defined as resisting Diotrephes and remaining loyal to John; and **doing evil** is here defined as siding with Diotrephes. John is not here writing a moral aphorism—he is moving to put down a rebellion.

St. John then commends **Demetrius** (probably the bearer of the letter). It is an emphatic commendation. Demetrius **has been witnessed to** as a good and devout man **by everyone** (that is, by all the Christians who know him). He has been witnessed to **by the truth itself** (that is, his whole life is self-evidently consistent with the truth of the apostolic faith). John himself and his own community **also witness**, and Gaius knows well enough that their **witness is true** and reliable. Thus there are three witnesses to Demetrius's worth (everyone, the truth itself, and John and his circle), and such a threefold witness is enough to establish the truth of it (compare Deut. 19:15; 1 John 5:8).

Why is such an impressive testimony given to Demetrius? It

seems a bit overdone for someone who is simply the carrier of a letter or who needs hospitality. Surely Gaius, famous for giving hospitality even to strangers (v. 5), would welcome in someone bringing a letter from the apostle John even without such a fulsome commendation.

I would suggest that the commendation of Demetrius is not meant primarily for Gaius, but for the larger church of Diotrephes. They are intended to see this letter, and John commends Demetrius so emphatically because he hopes the church there will expel Diotrephes and accept Demetrius in his place. The commendation of Demetrius reads like an invitation for the church's confirming cry of "*Axios!*" ("Worthy!"). It is the opening move for the housecleaning John will do when he comes.

§III.   Closing Words (13–14)

ॐ ॐ ॐ ॐ ॐ

13 I had many things to write to you, but I do not want to write them to you through ink and reed;

14 but I hope to see you immediately, and we will speak face to face. Peace *be* to you. The friends greet you. Greet the friends by name.

In St. John's closing words, he excuses himself for writing such a short letter to such a good friend. The brevity of the letter does not mean he has little to say to him. He actually has **many things to write** and share, but **hopes to see** Gaius **immediately**, when they can **speak face to face** (lit., "mouth to mouth"), enjoying the exchange of the living voice at great length. Until that time, this brief epistle will have to do.

John bids him **peace** (in good Jewish style) and says that **the friends greet** him. In return, he asks him to **greet the friends** there **by name**. That is, greetings are to be given to each one individually. One's name is important (compare the Good Shepherd calling each sheep by name; John 10:3), for each one has been redeemed by God and has inestimable value. Accordingly, John values each one of the friends; none of them are lost in the crowd.

John refers here to his supporters (both in his own city and in that of Gaius) as **friends** because of the close bonds uniting them. Friendship (rare today; a mere acquaintance is not a friend) imposes bonds of loyalty, and a friend will always stand by another friend. In the crisis of that time brought on by Diotrephes' rebellion, those bonds are all the more important. All who are friends in the truth of the Gospel must stand together.

About the Author

Archpriest Lawrence Farley currently pastors St. Herman of Alaska Orthodox Church (OCA) in Langley, B.C., Canada. He received his B.A. from Trinity College, Toronto, and his M.Div. from Wycliffe College, Toronto. A former Anglican priest, he converted to Orthodoxy in 1985 and studied for two years at St. Tikhon's Orthodox Seminary in Pennsylvania. In addition to the books in the Orthodox Bible Study Companion series, he has also published *The Christian Old Testament: Looking at the Hebrew Scriptures through Christian Eyes; A Song in the Furnace: The Message of the Book of Daniel; Unquenchable Fire: The Traditional Christian Teaching about Hell; A Daily Calendar of Saints: A Synaxarion for Today's North American Church; Let Us Attend: A Journey Through the Orthodox Divine Liturgy; One Flesh: Salvation through Marriage in the Orthodox Church; The Empty Throne: Reflections on the History and Future of the Orthodox Episcopacy;* and *Following Egeria: A Visit to the Holy Land through Time and Space.*

Visit www.ancientfaithradio.com to listen to Fr. Lawrence Farley's podcast, "The Coffee Cup Commentaries."

A Complete List of the Books in the Orthodox Bible Study Companion Series

The Gospel of Matthew
Torah for the Church
• Paperback, 400 pages, ISBN 978-0-9822770-7-2

The Gospel of Mark
The Suffering Servant
• Paperback, 280 pages, ISBN 978-1-888212-54-9

The Gospel of Luke
Good News for the Poor
• Paperback, 432 pages, ISBN 978-1-936270-12-5

The Gospel of John
Beholding the Glory
• Paperback, 376 pages, ISBN 978-1-888212-55-6

The Acts of the Apostles
Spreading the Word
• Paperback, 352 pages, ISBN 978-1-936270-62-0

The Epistle to the Romans
A Gospel for All
• Paperback, 208 pages, ISBN 978-1-888212-51-8

First and Second Corinthians
Straight from the Heart
• Paperback, 319 pages, ISBN 978-1-888212-53-2

Words of Fire
The Early Epistles of St. Paul to the Thessalonians and the Galatians
• Paperback, 172 pages, ISBN 978-1-936270-02-6

The Prison Epistles
Philippians – Ephesians – Colossians – Philemon
• Paperback, 224 pages, ISBN 978-1-888212-52-5

Shepherding the Flock
The Pastoral Epistles of St. Paul the Apostle to Timothy and Titus
• Paperback, 144 pages, ISBN 978-1-888212-56-3

The Epistle to the Hebrews
High Priest in Heaven
• Paperback, 184 pages, ISBN 978-1-936270-74-3

Universal Truth
The Catholic Epistles of James, Peter, Jude, and John
• Paperback, 232 pages, ISBN 978-1-888212-60-0

The Apocalypse of St. John
A Revelation of Love and Power
• Paperback, 240 pages, ISBN 978-1-936270-40-8

Other Books by the Author

The Christian Old Testament
Looking at the Hebrew Scriptures through Christian Eyes

Many Christians see the Old Testament as "the other Testament": a source of exciting stories to tell the kids, but not very relevant to the Christian life. *The Christian Old Testament* reveals the Hebrew Scriptures as the essential context of Christianity, as well as a many-layered revelation of Christ Himself. Follow along as Fr. Lawrence Farley explores the Christian significance of every book of the Old Testament.

• Paperback, 200 pages, ISBN 978-1-936270-53-8

A Song in the Furnace
The Message of the Book of Daniel

The Book of Daniel should be read with the eyes of a child. It's a book of wonders and extremes—mad kings, baffling dreams with gifted interpreters, breathtaking deliverances, astounding prophecies—with even what may be the world's first detective stories added in for good measure. To argue over the book's historicity, as scholars have done for centuries, is to miss the point. In *A Song in the Furnace*, Fr. Lawrence Farley reveals all the wonders of this unique book to the receptive eye.

• Paperback, 248 pages, ISBN 978-1-944967-31-4

Unquenchable Fire
The Traditional Christian Teaching about Hell

The doctrine of hell as a place of eternal punishment has never been easy for Christians to accept. The temptation to retreat from and reject the Church's traditional teaching about hell is particularly strong in our current culture, which has demonstrably lost its sense of sin. Fr. Lawrence Farley examines the Orthodox Church's teaching on this difficult subject through the lens of Scripture and patristic writings, making the case that the existence of hell does not negate that of a loving and forgiving God.unique book to the receptive eye.

• Paperback, 240 pages, ISBN 978-1-944967-18-5

A Daily Calendar of Saints
A Synaxarion for Today's North American Church

Fr. Lawrence Farley turns his hand to hagiography in this collection of lives of saints, one or more for each day of the calendar year. His accessible prose and contemporary approach make these ancient lives easy for modern Christians to relate to and understand.

• Paperback, 304 pages, ISBN 978-1-944967-41-3

Let Us Attend
A Journey Through the Orthodox Divine Liturgy

Fr. Lawrence Farley provides a guide to understanding the Divine Liturgy, and a vibrant reminder of the centrality of the Eucharist in living the Christian life, guiding believers in a devotional and historical walk through the Orthodox Liturgy. Examining the Liturgy section by section, he provides both historical explanations of how the Liturgy evolved and devotional insights aimed at helping us pray the Liturgy in the way the Fathers intended.

• Paperback, 104 pages, ISBN 978-1-888212-87-7

One Flesh
Salvation through Marriage in the Orthodox Church

Is the Church too negative about sex? Beginning with this provocative question, Fr. Lawrence Farley explores the history of the Church's attitude toward sex and marriage, from the Old Testament through the Church Fathers. He persuasively makes the case both for traditional morality and for a positive acceptance of marriage as a viable path to theosis.

• Paperback, 160 pages, ISBN 978-1-936270-66-8

The Empty Throne
Reflections on the History and Future of the Orthodox Episcopacy

In contemporary North America, the bishop's throne in the local parish stands empty for most of the year. The bishop is an honored occasional guest rather than a true pastor of the local flock. But it was not always so, nor need it be so forever. Fr. Lawrence Farley explores how the Orthodox episcopacy developed over the centuries and suggests what can be done in modern times to bring the bishop back into closer contact with his flock.

• Paperback, 152 pages, ISBN 978-1-936270-61-3

Following Egeria
A Visit to the Holy Land through Time and Space

In the fourth century, a nun named Egeria traveled through the Holy Land and wrote an account of her experiences. In the twenty-first century, Fr. Lawrence Farley followed partially in her footsteps and wrote his own account of how he experienced the holy sites as they are today. Whether you're planning your own pilgrimage or want to read about places you may never go, his account will inform and inspire you.

• Paperback, 160 pages, ISBN 978-1-936270-21-7

Other Books of Interest

The Orthodox Study Bible: Old and New Testaments

Featuring a Septuagint text of the Old Testament developed by outstanding
Orthodox scholars, this Bible also includes the complete Orthodox canon of
the Old Testament, including the Deuterocanon; insightful commentary drawn
from the Christian writers of the first ten centuries; helpful notes relating
Scripture to seasons of Christian feasting and fasting; a lectionary to guide your
Bible reading through the Church year; supplemental Bible study articles on
a variety of subjects; a subject index to the study notes to help facilitate Bible
study; and more.

• Available in various editions. Visite store.ancientfaith.com for more details.

Christ in the Psalms
by Patrick Henry Reardon

Avoiding both syrupy sentimentality and arid scholasticism, *Christ in the
Psalms* takes the reader on a thought-provoking and enlightening pilgrimage
through this beloved "Prayer Book" of the Church. Which psalms were quoted
most frequently in the New Testament, and how were they interpreted? How
has the Church historically understood and utilized the various psalms in her
liturgical life? How can we perceive the image of Christ shining through the
psalms? Lively and highly devotional, thought-provoking yet warm and practical, Christ in the Psalms sheds a world of insight upon each psalm, and offers
practical advice for how to make the Psalter a part of our daily lives.

• Paperback, 328 pages, ISBN 978-1-888212-21-7

The Rest of the Bible
A Guide to the Old Testament of the Early Church
by Theron Mathis

A beautiful widow risks her life to defend her people while men cower in fear.
A young man takes a journey with an archangel and faces down a demon in
order to marry a woman seven times widowed. A reprobate king repents and
miraculously turns back toward God. A Jewish exile plays a game of riddles in a
Persian king's court. Wisdom is detailed and exalted. Christ is revealed.

These and many other stories make up the collection of writings explored
in this book—authentic books of the Bible you've probably never read.
Dubbed "Apocrypha" and cut from the Bible by the Reformers, these books
of the Greek Old Testament were a vital part of the Church's life in the early
centuries, and are still read and treasured by Orthodox Christians today. *The
Rest of the Bible* provides a brief and intriguing introduction to each of these
valuable texts, which St. Athanasius termed "the Readables."

• Paperback, 128 pages, ISBN 978-1-936270-15-6

For complete ordering information, visit our website: store.ancientfaith.com.